National Children's Bureau series

Editor: Mia Kellmer Pringle

This new series examines contemporary issues relating to the development of children and their needs in the family, school and society. Based on recent research and taking account of current practice, it also discusses policy implications for the education, health and social services. The series is relevant not only for professional workers, administrators, researchers and students but also for parents and those involved in self-help movements and consumer groups.

Combined Nursery Centres
Elsa Ferri, Dorothy Birchall,
Virginia Gingell and Caroline Gipps

Children in Changing Families: a Study of Adoption and Illegitimacy
Lydia Lambert and Jane Streather

Caring for Separated Children
R. A. Parker (editor)

A Fairer Future for Children
Mia Kellmer Pringle

Unqualified and Underemployed: Handicapped Young People and the Labour Market
Alan Walker

Unqualified and Underemployed

Handicapped Young People and the Labour Market

Alan Walker

First published 1982 by
THE MACMILLAN PRESS LTD
London and Basingstoke
Companies and representatives
throughout the world

ISBN 0 333 32189 8 (hard cover)
ISBN 0 333 32190 1 (paper cover)

Typeset in 10/12pt Times by
ILLUSTRATED ARTS

Printed in Hong Kong

For Carol

Contents

viii *Contents*

Acknowledgements

Many people gave advice and helpful comments over the course of the research and the preparation of this book. I would like to thank first all of my former colleagues at the National Children's Bureau for the help and assistance they gave the research team over the two years of this project. It was a privilege to work with such kind and generous people. At various stages of the research Roy Evans, Ken Fogelman, Dougal Hutchison and Peter Wedge made particularly helpful suggestions. The computing and statistical help of Bob Wellburn, Helen Smith, Vanessa Chestney and especially Jenny Head was invaluable. Other members of the Bureau, too numerous to mention, also gave support and advice over the course of the research. The detailed and cogent comments made by Mia Pringle and Peter Wedge resulted in significant improvements in the manuscript. Their guidance is gratefully acknowledged and any remaining defects are entirely mine.

Kath Downing, Roz Treadway, Joyce Famosa and Esther Mason at the National Children's Bureau typed the first draft; while Alice Gavins, Christine Bell, Jeanette Leaman and Sheila Fuller at the Department of Sociological Studies, University of Sheffield, and Caroline Simonds at the National Children's Bureau typed the final manuscript. Both of these difficult tasks were carried out with great efficiency.

As well as gratefully acknowledging the support of the Department of Education and Science for the research on which this book is based, I would like to thank members of the Warnock Committee liaison group for the helpful suggestions and comments given at important points in the research. John Fish, John Hedger, Imogen Luxton, David Hutchinson and Philip Williams asked searching questions and kept us on our toes throughout the two years. The

University of Sheffield generously provided some financial support for the preparations of the manuscript for publication. The Inner London Education Authority and Northumberland County Education Authority kindly provided small samples of young people for the pilot studies.

In view of the scope and nature of the research, two years is a very short period. Consequently the researchers were under constant and considerable pressure, particularly in the latter stages when there were various delays beyond our control. My research colleague Patricia Stapenhurst withstood this pressure magnificently and tackled every research task with equal commitment and zeal. Without her invaluable help and dedication this project could not have been completed.

I owe an enormous debt to the 500 young people and their parents who kindly gave up long periods of their time to enable the research to be carried out. I hope that some of this kindness may be repaid by policy measures in response to this book and the report of the Warnock Committee to improve the conditions and life-chances of the handicapped. Finally, this book is dedicated to Carol, without whose love and support it could not have been written.

University of Sheffield   Alan Walker

1

Introduction

Disadvantage and the labour market

> I think if you can't read and write they should ask you questions, because I am quite bright if they ask me questions, but I am just a dead loss when it comes to putting it down on paper. They should have more practical stuff instead of all this paper work.

This quotation, a clear cry from the heart, exposes one of the fundamental weaknesses of modern industrial societies. Educational systems, with the apparent aim of equal opportunity, become geared to providing for the most able, who through examination results and qualifications gain entry to employment or higher education: what Titmuss called 'the spread of credentialism'.[1] This inevitably creates a pool of educational 'failures'. Although special educational provision may be made for the least able, 'success' in employment rests primarily on paper qualifications. The labour market and educational systems have come to reflect each other in a hierarchical way, the latter being organised to supply the former. Paradoxically the spread of universal education may have created as many barriers as it destroyed. The market value of education overshadows its other values. Entrance to employment above the unskilled level becomes more and more difficult as professional and other bureaucratic groupings demand more and more educational qualifications. In such a world the unqualified are largely doomed to the 'failure' of unrewarding work:

> Well, at one factory we saw things and one part would be noisy and another part would be too dirty; and then at another factory it would be too quiet – it would drive us batty. It showed us some

things we wouldn't like to do. I thought that then, but now I wouldn't mind doing anything as long as I was working.

The second quotation, like the first, from an 'educationally subnormal (moderate)' — abbreviated ESN(M) — young man, highlights a number of factors which are reported in this book. Handicapped young people are, in general, a disadvantaged minority in the labour market. They have access to a very restricted range of jobs; they frequently work in poor conditions, in dirty, noisy and repetitive jobs, but most importantly in the current economic climate they are even more likely than the non-handicapped to be unemployed and have difficulty in finding work.

The primary aim of this book is to report information hitherto not available in this country, on the conditions that handicapped young people encounter on entering the labour market, and their experiences during the first two years of their working life. The research on which it is based was concentrated on the responses of young people themselves (and their parents) to the transition from school to labour market, rather than on the views of the experts in the fields of education and careers guidance. In addition, small studies were carried out amongst headmasters and, uniquely to this research, employers (see Chapters 10 and 13).

The research was commissioned for the Committee of Enquiry into the Education of Handicapped Children and Young People (Warnock Committee),[2] and a report on it was submitted in October 1977. The survey was carried out in 1976 amongst a nationally representative sample of 500 young people, most of whom were handicapped, and samples of parents, employers and headteachers. The young people were all 18 years old when interviewed, and geographically spread throughout Britain.

Educational handicap and employment

The term 'handicap' is used here and subsequently in the special sense of *educational* handicap. Thus all the young people had either been classified or *ascertained* as needing special educational help at age 16; or had been receiving such help though not formally classified; or were thought to have needed special help. (Definitions are given in Chapter 2.) In addition there was a small 'control group' of non-handicapped young people. This definition of handicap is therefore much broader than classifications based on impairment, such as blindness or cerebral palsy, or functional restriction based on the assessment of physical capacity only.[3] Similarly the Department of Employment's Disabled Persons Register, administered under the Disabled Persons (Employment) Act 1944 is open to all disabled people who are employable and *substantially* handicapped. In practice the register has been dominated by people with physical disabilities (in contrast to some other European countries such as Holland, Sweden and Denmark).[4]

Therefore, the register seriously underestimates the number of handicapped young people.[5] Only a minority of young people classified as 'handicapped' in this study had observable physical impairments, which marked them as different from other 18-year-olds. Herein lies one of the main problems facing the educationally handicapped young person in the labour market. There is a wide range of special provisions for the severely handicapped, which though by no means wholly adequate recognise to some extent in policy and practice that these handicaps present important employment problems. Employment services for the much larger group of educationally handicapped people are virtually non-existent except for the provision of just over 100 posts for specialist careers officers to deal with the handicapped throughout Britain. In addition, employers often do not recognise the special needs and problems of these young people (see Chapter 10).

The treatment of special educational needs within the school system increases the contrast between school and work. Educationally subnormal pupils, by definition, receive some special form of education, usually within the setting of a special school. As the authors of an Inner London Education Authority (ILEA) survey of handicapped school-leavers note, the transition from school to work for an educationally handicapped young person can be a more significant change than that experienced by other leavers: 'With this emphasis on educational retardation there are school-leavers entering an adult world where to be educationally subnormal is not a recognised condition and where opportunities must generally be sought in non-specialist provision.'[6] This problem is exacerbated when young people suffer from some emotional instability which may have more impact on their behaviour than educational backwardness (and may often be the cause of the latter). Thus employers and workmates witnessing 'bad' or erratic behaviour may be more inclined to sack or further antagonise the young person, rather than make allowances for and seek advice about the problem (see Chapters 8 and 9).

In the transition from school to work, the existence of a special problem at school may be overlooked or forgotten until it manifests itself at the workplace. This is particularly true for those with learning or behaviour difficulties, which are easiest to conceal. Careers officers in trying to further the interests of the young person, may unwittingly exacerbate the latter's difficulty by not revealing details of the special nature of the young person's problems. Such problems do not cease to exist when young people leave school and they may need special help and support in employment as well (see Chapter 7).

The scope of special education

The numerical importance of special education was underlined recently by the Warnock Committee. It estimated that about one in six children at any time – as many as 1.6 million children – and up to one in five children at some time in their school lives will need some form of special educational provision.[7] The forms that this provision may take are varied and differ between authorities. This spectrum of special educational provision covers four groups: special schools catering wholly or mainly for handicapped pupils; special units or classes attached to ordinary schools, part-time special or 'remedial' classes in ordinary schools and full-time education in ordinary classes with additional help.[8]

ESN(M) children predominate in the representative sample of handicapped young people in this study. This category of handicap includes a wide range of abilities and, as the Department of Education and Science (DES) Schools Inspectorate has noted, they 'are not always clearly distinguishable from the much larger group of slower pupils of the ordinary schools'.[9] The IQ range in ILEA special day schools for ESN(M) young people is 50 – 85 per cent. Forty-four per cent of these people have an IQ of more than 70 per cent.[10] The Handicapped Pupils and Special School Regulations 1959, define 'educationally subnormal pupils' as pupils who by reason of limited ability or other conditions resulting in educational retardation require some specialised form of education wholly or partly in substitution for the education normally given in ordinary schools.[11] Thus for whatever reason, physical or mental impairment, learning difficulty, loss of schooling, social or environmental background, ESN(M) children consistently have lower educational achievements than their peers.

Although a change of the label 'educational subnormality' may have the effect of reducing the stigma that many young people and their parents feel – in 1967 the Plowden Report suggested 'slow learner', in 1972 the National Union of Teachers used 'educationally handicapped', and in 1978 the Warnock Committee proposed 'children with learning difficulties'[12] – the fact remains that the young people are classified as educational failures, partly because they do not enter the labour market with even minimal qualifications. Although some three-fifths of school-leavers in Great Britain leave school without at least one GCE 'O' level or CSE pass at grades A to C or one CSE pass at grade 1, and many of them have passes at lower grades, there is still a substantial minority without any qualifications.[13]

In addition these young people face the stigma of knowing, themselves, that they have been classed as educationally backward. Society confirms their failure by the status they occupy on entering the labour market (see Chapter 4) and by the denial of a second chance through further education and training (see Chapter 11) while at the same time channelling huge resources to the educationally most able in the higher education sector. This brings us to the central concern of this book: the effect of educational handicap on labour market experiences and achievements. It is known that certain groups of school-leavers are at a disadvantage in the job market, but the dimensions of this disadvantage and its cause have not been adequately explored hitherto.

Disadvantage and employment

It can be assumed that all handicapped people are at a disadvantage in the labour market, but while this may in general be true, the Warnock Committee point out that there is no 'simple relationship between handicap in educational terms and the severity of a disability in medical terms for a disadvantage in social terms'.[14] The majority of children ascertained as educationally handicapped are physically fit, healthy and mobile. They are 'backward' in the sense of being held back; their learning ability has been restricted by various environmental, social and anatomical factors.[15] On the basis of Passow's definition they are all *disadvantaged*. Thus, 'A child is *disadvantaged* if, because of social, or cultural characteristics. . . he comes into the school system with knowledge, skills and attitudes which impede learning and contribute to a cumulative academic deficit.'[16]

'Disadvantage' is a relative concept and the size and nature of the group in question will differ according to the social context. For example, if the ESN(M) school leaver is disadvantaged in applying for a job as a shop assistant, then he is also likely to be disadvantaged along with his non-handicapped but unqualified peer in applying for a job as a solicitors' clerk, compared with a non-handicapped leaver with five 'O' levels. But the ESN(M) leaver in this example is *consistently* at a disadvantage, and it is in this sense that I am employing the term 'disadvantage in the labour market' here. It applies to that group of young people whose personal and social (including educational) attributes are counted as adverse characteristics, implicitly or explicitly, by different employers in the labour market. The result is that they are consistently near the end of every queue for jobs.

A judgement of success or failure in a career or trade is obviously premature after only 2 years in the labour market. This book is therefore confined to an examination of success or failure in getting and keeping jobs in relation to other young people at a similar stage of development. This investigation therefore raises important questions about the role of work in industrial societies (obviously the problem of educational handicap is tiny in such societies compared with the Third World) and the social distribution of life chances, that can only be considered in outline (see Chapter 9). Experiences in the labour market, success and failure, advantage and disadvantage, depend primarily on the social construction of the division of labour and the significance attached to work in different societies.

Work is of fundamental importance to the survival of industrial societies and it is not surprising therefore that there are powerful sanctions exerted against the unemployed, through formal institutionalised social security systems or through informal social relationships. The workplace in industrial societies provides a significant focal point for personal evaluation. As Eliot Liebow argues 'To be denied work is to be denied far more than the things that paid work buys; it is to be denied the ability to define and respect one's self.'[17] The economic system is legitimated in one way through the process of blaming the victims for their own circumstances. As a result individuals without work or those working in low status jobs, are likely to experience anxiety and other problems or alienation, but do not go so far as to question the economic system or the structure of social relationships which shape their lives.[18] Thus handicapped young people who are unemployed or in unskilled jobs are a passive minority, powerless and unlikely to question publicly the injustice that their disadvantage represents.[19] Whatever future employment prospects are for all manual workers in the age of the silicon chip, handicapped young and older people are likely to remain a disadvantaged minority and to be among the first to suffer in any contraction of job opportunities (see Chapter 4).

Young people are not the most disadvantaged group in the labour market, because older workers, disabled people and ethnic minorities tend to be more vulnerable to long-term unemployment. But there does appear to be a job crisis, in the British economy, that will particularly affect the employment opportunities of handicapped school-leavers. This is obvious from the unemployment statistics showing 46 000 unemployed school leavers in January 1980 and 290 000 in July.[20]

But less obvious is the fact that part of the downturn in demand for young people which these statistics reflect, is likely to be permanent, rather than cyclical.[21] For example, there has been a loss of many 'dead-end' jobs such as junior messengers and office boys and more disturbing still, of junior operative posts in engineering firms, which were often the route to skilled jobs.[22] It is precisely these kinds of unskilled and semi-skilled jobs that handicapped young people have been occupying in times of fuller employment. Growth and reflation alone, therefore, cannot overcome their disadvantage. In a recession, disadvantage in the labour market is emphasised. Success in gaining employment depends primarily on the availability of jobs both nationally and locally, but when job opportunities are reduced, they are rationed by the interaction of employers' demands and the characteristics of those in the market for labour (see Chapter 10).

Young people and the dual labour market

Is there a separate labour market for young people?[23] First, what do I mean by the term 'labour market'? Robertson has defined labour markets as 'the mechanisms, principally institutional, by which employers (as buyers of labour) and workers and their representatives (as sellers of labour) can affect the employment and utilisation of manpower.'[24] Robinson defines them more specifically as the activity of luring labour and the determination of job descriptions and remuneration.[25] Throughout this book the term 'labour market' is taken to mean all the social relationships and institutions through which people obtain jobs.

Robinson has also distinguished internal and external labour markets, or processes for the hiring of labour. Clearly there is not a national labour market but a large number of local ones, some of which may be dominated by single firms. For certain kinds of jobs, particularly professional and managerial jobs, there is only a national system of job recruitment. Most manual workers who tend not to be geographically mobile are dependent on job opportunities in their immediate locality. They depend on formal and informal communication networks for learning about such openings. The former include the Careers Service and Jobcentres, and the latter, friends and relatives.

Some of the different labour markets correspond broadly to certain models of operation and practice. Thus there is similarity between firms in the recruitment, training, pay and conditions experienced by different workers according to their skill-level and status, and according to the level of union activity. It has been suggested that there are two main forms of labour market: a 'primary' high wage sector and a 'secondary' low wage sector. Dual labour market theory suggests that the effects of low education and discrimination (according to race or colour) are cumulative, and that disparity between the incomes of advantaged and disadvantaged workers may widen following labour market entry, as a result of different job training, job changing and career patterns.[26] The theory posits two distinct labour market careers: firstly, where a genuine 'career' is followed by one group and job changes are made only to secure promotion, and secondly where the disadvantaged remain concentrated in dead-end jobs, with little training or upward career mobility. These may usefully be conceptualised as two models at opposite ends of a *continuum* of labour market experiences. Unemployment is concentrated among the disadvantaged in the secondary labour markets. 'Low wage employment is dead-end, leading to little on-the-job training and economic advancement, and certain groups of workers – the less well-educated, women and ethnic minorities – tend to congregate in these jobs for long periods of time.'[27]

Secondary labour markets become associated with certain kinds of workers such as frequent job changers (see Chapter 9). High turnover characterises secondary labour markets, but job changes may be voluntary and involuntary.[28] These models of labour markets and labour market careers are, of course, oversimplifications. Different firms recruit labour in different ways. The attitude of individual employers or the existence of strong unions as well as the experiences of individual young people, may significantly alter this general pattern.[29] But in general, if a firm or business requires unskilled labour it will fill the jobs through external recruitment and offer minimum training. If high levels of skill or specialised skills related to a particular product or process are required, the firm is more likely to invest in training and internal promotion. Thus it is skill-level that primarily determines recruitment and training; therefore the different forms of labour market and experiences that go with them usually coexist in the same firm or business.

Although this research did not set out to test the validity of the dual labour market thesis, it can be usefully borne in mind through-out the ensuing analysis, firstly, because it provides one framework for the examination of the labour market experiences of handicapped young people and secondly, because it suggests certain policies to combat their disadvantage including training and job development (see Chapters 5 and 11).

Handicapped and careerless

The main dual labour market thesis is that low education and discrimination interact to place disadvantaged workers on relatively dead-end earnings paths in contrast to the upwardly mobile income paths available to more advantaged workers. The majority of handicapped young people do not have 'careers' in the generally accepted sense of a progressive advancement in job status, they are 'careerless'.[30] Furthermore, whilst it may be valid to consider non-manual and professional jobs in terms of choice, the notion of a free choice of occupations for these low-skilled young workers is totally erroneous (see Chapter 7). The life-chances and employment status of most young people are determined prior to labour market entry, by family, class and educational background (see Chapter 13).[31] Although it may be argued that a period of two years in the labour market is too soon to assess the employment experiences of young people, there is a great deal of evidence to suggest that the individual's first job is an excellent indication of what his last job will be.[32]

Previous research on school-leavers has tended to concentrate on careers advice and occupational choice;[33] on adjustment to employment rather than on the objective conditions of work and the structure of opportunity within different labour markets. The experience of young and older workers is dependent upon their position within the class structure of society, and for those in the lowest classes this means that they can exercise very little control over many decisions which affect their lives. In this sense their position embodies alienation.[34] In the following analyses the individual experiences of the 18-year-olds in the sample are assessed as far as possible in the light of the overall structure of opportunity rather than simply in individualistic terms. The problems of handicapped school-leavers require special policies (see Chapter 14) but they also share common problems with other unskilled young workers, for example, insecure employment and poor working conditions, which cannot be overlooked in attempting to counteract their disadvantage. For many handicapped young people, as the following quotation illustrates, the experience of school is an unhappy one; 'I didn't like school very much. People used to take the mickey out of me because I couldn't write very good. So once I could leave I was glad to finish.' Can we account for this rejection of school by young people solely in terms of individual behaviour or attitudes? 'Far from being irrational or disfunctional it can be argued that such rejection is necessary for those who are already, or are about to be, defined as failures in terms of the educational performance criteria accepted by those who control and operate the educational system.'[35]

Subsequent analysis which details the disadvantage suffered by many handicapped school leavers, suggests that society is failing a significant and growing proportion of its citizens and so is underutilising its natural resources. More importantly, it is unfairly imposing the burden of its failure to provide sufficient work of a rewarding kind on only a few groups in society, at the same time strongly denigrating those without work. They are bearing, in Titmuss's words, 'the cost of other people's progress'.[36] A society which does not share its social costs more evenly does not justify the epithets 'developed' or 'welfare state', still less if it embodies structures which create a disadvantaged minority to bear this burden of unemployment and poor employment conditions.

The main dimensions of comparison used in this book are educational ability, the educational failures and successes, and social class, based on the young person's occupation. In addition two main variables are constructed to classify labour market experiences (see Chapters 7 and 9). Chapter 2 describes the research methods used in the investigation and sketches the general background to the study. Chapter 3 concentrates on some of the individual experiences of young people in the survey told largely in their own words. The results of the analyses of different aspects of their labour market experiences are presented in subsequent chapters.

Periodically reference is made in the text to supplementary tables. These contain further information to that provided in the book and are available from:

> The Supplementary Publications Division,
> (Reference SUP 81009),
> British Library (Lending Division),
> Walton,
> Boston Spa,
> Wetherby,
> Yorkshire LS23 7BQ

Also available from the same source are two appendices, 'Analysis of response' (Appendix 1) and 'Assessing the severity of disability' (Appendix 2).

2

Scope and Nature of the Research

There is a dearth of information about employment opportunities for and work experiences of handicapped school-leavers. The major studies of school-leavers in Britain have not dealt with the special problems of the handicapped[1] and the few that have investigated this aspect of the transition from school to work have been concerned predominantly with the experiences and needs of groups of young people with specific impairments or handicapping conditions. The most notable have been studies of young people with cardiac disabilities and mental retardation[2] hearing impairments[3] and blindness.[4] Only one national study has taken a broader approach – an investigation, carried out in 1971, of leavers from all types of special schools.[5] But a major limitation of that important research was that information was obtained from young people or their parents by careers officers rather than by more independent means. Another recent study of handicapped and non-handicapped school leavers was confined to one locality.[6] Thus, prior to the study reported here, no recent research into the employment position of handicapped young people had been based on information collected from a nationally representative sample.

The Warnock Committee decided that the National Child Development Study (NCDS) was an excellent starting point for such an inquiry since it provided not only an identified sample of young people, many of whom had been in the labour market for nearly two years, but also a wide range of developmental and other information collected at previous follow-ups. The NCDS has studied the progress of all the children born in Britain in one week in March 1958. Information had been obtained on over 17 000 babies. There were subsequent follow-ups at ages 7, 11 and 16.[7] The third and most recent main follow-up was carried out in 1974 when the young people were in their last year of compulsory education.

Warnock Committee

On 22 November 1973, a committee chaired by Mrs Mary Warnock was appointed by the Secretary of State for Education and Science, with the following terms of reference:

> to review education provision in England, Scotland and Wales for children and young people handicapped by disabilities of body or mind, taking account of the medical aspects of their needs, together with arrangements to prepare them for entry into employment; to consider the most effective use of resources for these purposes, and to make recommendations.

The Committee started work the following year, holding its first meeting in September 1974.[8] In its first year the Warnock Committee divided into four sub-committees, covering: the needs of handicapped children under five; the education of handicapped children in ordinary schools; day special schools and boarding provision, and the education and other needs of handicapped school leavers. This research was commissioned by the last-named sub-committee. The project began on 1 October, 1975, and lasted for two years.

Definition of special educational treatment

The main definition of handicap used by the NCDS, and therefore the starting point for a definition of handicap in this research, is educational handicap; that is, the need for special educational treatment. At the follow-up of 16-year-olds, a total of 3 per cent of those who had been medically examined, had been ascertained as being in need of special education, because of educational backwardness or some emotional or physical handicap.[9] Response bias implied that this was likely to be a slight underestimate. Before proceeding to describe the construction of the sample it is necessary, firstly, to define the terms 'ascertainment' and 'special educational treatment'; and secondly, to consider official classifications of educational handicap.

Special educational treatment is defined, in institutional terms, by Section 8(2)(c) of the Education Act 1944, as 'education by special methods appropriate for persons suffering from disability of mind and/or body'. It may be provided 'either in special schools or otherwise'. The term 'ascertainment' was used in Section 34(1) of the 1944 Education Act and 'is the whole process of determining which children require special education'.[10] Under Section 34 of the Education Act, local education authorities were given, and still have, a statutory duty 'to ascertain what children in their area require special educational treatment'.[11] Previously this duty had been confined to 'defective' and 'epileptic' children.

The Handicapped Pupils and School Health Service Regulations, 1945, defined eleven categories of handicapped pupils: blind, partially sighted, deaf, partially deaf, delicate, diabetic, educationally subnormal, epileptic, physically handicapped, maladjusted and those with speech defects. The last two were new categories. These categories have remained largely unchanged since 1944 (in 1953 diabetic children were included with delicate children) but their precise definitions have been altered, most recently by the Handicapped Pupils and Special Schools Regulations, 1959, made under Section 33 of the 1944 Act. Blind, deaf, epileptic and physically handicapped children were considered sufficiently severely handicapped to be required to be educated in special schools, while those with other disabilities could attend ordinary schools if provision was made for them. It was estimated in 1944 that between 14 per cent and 17 per cent of the school population would eventually need special educational treatment.

The educationally subnormal were those children of limited ability and those retarded by 'other conditions', such as irregular attendance at school, ill-health, lack of continuity in their education or unsatisfactory school conditions. Today the ESN(M) are the largest group of children in special schools and are also a large proportion of those in ordinary schools receiving special help (in units attached to ordinary schools or in remedial groups). According to the Warnock Committee such learning difficulties may stem from physical or sensory disability, poor social or educational background, a specific learning difficulty or limited general ability.[12] Maladjustment is most difficult to define and encompasses children with emotional and behavioural disorders. 'Such disorders spring from many causes, including difficult home circumstances, adverse temperamental characteristics and brain dysfunction.'[13]

Under the Education (Handicapped Children) Act, 1970, mentally handicapped or 'mentally deficient' children became entitled to special education and were labelled as severely educationally sub-normal, ESN(S), as distinct from the *moderately* educationally sub-normal, ESN(M), who had previously been classified as ESN. And under Circular 15/70 junior training centres became special schools.[14] Intelligence tests continue to be used in the determination of need for special education.

Having commented previously on the relationship between handicap and disadvantage, and on the limitation of ascertainment as a formal definition of handicap, it is necessary to note further drawbacks to the official definition of educational handicap. Three important deficiencies result, primarily, from local variations in policy and especially on the availability of special provision. The proportion of children ascertained as being in need of special education varies widely between local authorities. Thus in England and Wales, in January 1977, the prevalence of children ascertained as requiring special education ranged from below 120 per 10 000 of the school population in some predominantly rural authorities to above 300 in a small number of counties with large conurbations. In over one-half of the 105 authorities the ascertainment rate was more than 10 per cent above or below the average of 183.[15] Secondly, the ascertainment of children with particular handicaps varies even more widely within authorities. Thus, according to the report of the Warnock Committee, in one London borough in January 1977, ten times as many children were ascertained as maladjusted as in another borough. Thirdly, the problem of special educational need is much wider than official data suggest. Some schools set up special classes outside the formal provision of special education. In 1976, 10 845 such classes were attached to as many schools in England and Wales (nearly 40 per cent of all maintained primary, middle, and secondary schools) making, mostly part-time, provision for 494 248 pupils.[16] Such drawbacks to the use of a definition of handicap based on formal educational provision were reduced in this research by the inclusion of broader categories of educational handicap and disadvantage, in addition to the official classifications.

The population of handicapped young people

In January 1977, 133 609 handicapped pupils (age 2 to over 19) were receiving full-time tuition in special schools.[17] Some 21 393 were assessed as requiring special educational treatment during 1975 and 22 574 were newly placed in special schools or boarding homes. In all 176 688 handicapped pupils in England and Wales (1.8 per cent of the school population) were ascertained as needing *separate special educational provision.* Over 40 000 (nearly one-quarter) were either attending special classes in ordinary schools (18 667 full-time and 2003 part-time), receiving education else-where (for example, home tuition) or were awaiting entry to special schools. (Of the 9313 in this last category, 3244 had been awaiting admission for more than a year.) Two-thirds of all ascertained pupils are educationally subnormal – with 46 per cent classified as ESN(M).

DES figures underestimate the extent of handicap amongst young people age 16 or under, since only those who have been for-mally ascertained are included. There are large numbers of children in need of special educational provision but not receiving it. Fur-thermore, DES figures cannot be used to estimate numbers *over* 16, beyond those ascertained who stay on at school (one percent of the special school population). As the vast majority do not stay on at school, we must look to information provided by independent studies to get a broad picture of the prevalance of educational handicap.

One important source of information on the prevalence of handicaps amongst children is the National Child Development Study (NCDS). At the age of 16 years 3 per cent of the 17 000 young people studied were ascertained as being in need of special educa-tion (1.9 per cent were in special schools). Of those attending ordi-nary schools (approximately 16 670) 7 per cent were receiving special help within the school because of educational or mental backwardness, 5 per cent because of behavioural difficulties and 1 per cent because of a physical or sensory disability. Special help in school was considered desirable by their teachers for a further 5.5 per cent.[18] Moreover because of the omission of some young people from the follow-up it is likely that this is an under-estimate. It is clear that the concept of educational handicap covers a significant section of the school population, at least one in six children, and that a study of their first experiences of work was long over due.

Sample and research methods

The sample of 18-year-olds in this study was selectively drawn from the NCDS. Information at each of the three main NCDS follow-ups was collected by means of three questionnaires (four were used at 16) and a test booklet. Different questionnaires were completed by teachers, parents, the school medical service, and, at 16, the young people themselves.[19]

A preliminary analysis of the data after the follow-up of 16-year-olds revealed a total of 596 young people who had *ever* been ascertained as handicapped, 363 of them still being ascertained at age 16. The numbers in different groups were: 327 ESN(M), 52 ESN(S), 112 maladjusted and 146 physically handicapped. In addition to those formally ascertained as handicapped, there were 478 16-year-olds who, in view of their teachers, would have benefited from special help at school. This included help for educational or mental backwardness, behaviour difficulties and physical or sensory handicaps, the majority being in the first two groups. There were also 946 young people who were not ascertained but who were receiving some special help within school.

Due to financial as well as methodological constraints the size of the final sample had to be limited. It was decided that the aims of the survey would be best served if those who had been ascertained and had previously received special education but were no longer receiving it when they were 16 were excluded (234 young people). The selected sample of 18-year-olds comprised the following four main groups:

(i) *The handicapped group.* Those young people formally ascertained as needing special education at age 16. The largest number in the sample were ESN(M). It will be immediately apparent that the range of handicaps in this group is wide, encompassing the ESN(S) young person with the IQ below 50, the wheelchair-bound physically handicapped child and the young person with learning or behaviour difficulties. Furthermore the 'physically handicapped' includes the blind and partially sighted, deaf and partially hearing, delicate, epileptic, autistic and those with speech defects.

(ii) *The special help group.* Consisting of those young people receiving help for educational backwardness at 16, but who were not formally ascertained. This was the group reported by their teachers as having received special help within the school because of educational or mental backwardness. This help may or may not have been adequate in the view of the teacher and largely depended on the facilities of the school. This group extended the definition of 'handicap' to include those who were, in practice, identified by the ordinary school as such and getting special help. There were nearly 600 such children in the NCDS follow-up of 16-year-olds.

(iii) *The would benefit group.* The NCDS 'would benefit' group comprised those not formally ascertained, nor receiving any special help at 16 (as in (ii)), but who, in the opinion of their teacher, would have benefited from such provision because of educational or mental backwardness, educational or mental superiority, behaviour difficulties or any physical or sensory disability. The total number in one or more of these groups at 16 was about 500. As the majority were in the first group we sampled only from this group. At 7 years the classification of this group was largely attributed to 'adverse social or environmental factors'. Only about one-fifth had any physical abnormality and mental backwardness accounted for the vast majority.[20]

(iv) *The non-handicapped group.* This control group consisted of those *not* ascertained or receiving or needing (in the opinion of teachers) any special help for educational backwardness, behavioural difficulties, physical or sensory disability at 16 years. This group was selected in order to enable a comparative analysis to be carried out with the handicapped group.

Thus the sample was stratified disproportionately, according to three different definitions of educational handicap; formal ascertainment, practice and opinion; and therefore covered an extremely wide spectrum of abilities. This was done to allow the inclusion of all the formally ascertained handicapped in the final sample, as well as roughly equal numbers in the other sample groups (see Table 2.1).

The handicapped group was the only sample group in which random sampling was *not* carried out. Thus it included all young people who had ever been ascertained as ESN(S), all young people ascertained as maladjusted or as having physical/sensory handicaps at 16 years, and all those ascertained as ESN(M) at 16 years. Where a young person was ascertained as being both physically handicapped and ESN(M) he or she was included in the 'physically handicapped' group. On the other hand, a person both ESN(M) and maladjusted was, for our purpose, counted amongst the ESN(M). A further group, the ESN(M) at 11 years, included the other young people ascertained at 11 years: some of these have since been de-ascertained, whilst for others there were not data at 16 years.

TABLE 2.1 *Composition of the final sample*

Sample group		Number	Percentage
(i)	ESN(S)	43	8.5
	Physically handicapped	36	7.1
	ESN(M)	152	31.3
	Maladjusted	34	5.3
(ii)	Special help	72	14.2
(iii)	Would benefit	56	11.0
(iv)	Non-handicapped	115	22.6
Total		508	100

The survey

The main interview schedule was tested and revised on the basis of two pilot studies, in areas with different employment situations, one in London, the other in Northumberland.[21] For the main survey initial postal contact was made by the research team with over 850 young people, seeking permission to pass on their names and addresses to the fieldwork organisation. These young people are referred to subsequently as the *original sample*. At this first stage 20 per cent refused to take part, despite the fact that this involved returning a 'refusal' slip. Those who were willing to be interviewed were not required to respond by post. Some other young people had moved, so after some of these were traced, 640 addresses were issued to interviewers at the end of May 1976. This group of young people comprised the *actual, or issued sample*.

Tracing current addresses for members of the sample presented problems not encountered in previous NCDS follow-ups, when addresses were obtained from the schools. The majority of the sample had been out of school for two years. During this time many had moved house, so that the addresses available to the researchers were sometimes out of date. Considerable efforts were made to trace young people, involving careers officers, social workers, doctors and past employers. In a few cases parents were traced who did not know the whereabouts of their son or daughter.

The fieldwork was organised by Social and Community Planning Research (SCPR) and carried out by the Centre for Sample Surveys. Interviewers were briefed during May 1976 and detailed instructions were also issued to each interviewer, giving explanatory notes on most questions. There were considerable delays in the fieldwork stage and some questionnaires were still filtering back in October and November. In addition to the main survey, two small follow-ups of headmasters and employers were also carried out and these are reported in Chapters 11 and 14.

Response to the survey

The validity of any survey results depends partly on the percentage of the sample who are actually contacted, but primarily on the representativeness of that percentage who are finally interviewed. The proportion contacted from the *total* sample drawn from the NCDS (excluding those who had died or emigrated, were untraced and for whom addresses were not issued) was 64 per cent, while the response rate for the sample finally issued to interviewers was 82 per cent.

The non-responders can be classified into different groups according to the reason why they were not interviewed. This is discussed fully in a statistical Appendix which, like the Supplementary Tables, is available from the British Library (Lending Division).[22] The vast majority of those young people who refused to take part in the research dropped out when they were first contacted, by letter. The percentage of young people who refused to be interviewed at the fieldwork stage was relatively small. Thirty-eight per cent had changed their addresses and could not be contacted. There was considerable variation in response rate between the different groups in the sample with 81 per cent of the original sample of ESN(S) young people responding compared with 54 per cent among the 'would benefit' group.[23]

Some indication of the difficulty of obtaining interviews with young people, and handicapped young people in particular, can be gained from an analysis of the percentage of the original sample for whom there was data collected at the third NCDS follow-up, when the young person was age 16 and still at school. For the Individual Questionnaire, the average response rate among the handicapped group was 71 per cent. This latter figure excludes the ESN(S) among whom only 6 per cent were capable of completing the questionnaire. There were differences between the other handicap groups, ranging from 89 per cent of the physically handicapped to 75 per cent of the ESN(M). The proportion of the non-handicapped interviewed was 71 per cent.

Despite the difficulties of obtaining interviews with handicapped school leavers, the results of previous research indicate that the response rate obtained in this survey was good. For example, in the research on handicapped young people carried out at the National Children's Bureau by Linda Tuckey and her colleagues, youth employment records were available for 67 per cent of the 1373 eligible school leavers: 58 per cent of the 1373 were interviewed and 25 per cent of employers were interviewed.[24] In her study of school leavers Joan Maizels contacted 240 firms, received replies from 100 (42 per cent) and 57 (25 per cent) agreed to take part in the research.[25]

Sample bias

It was important to know whether there were any biases in the final sample, and a detailed analysis was carried out to compare the responders and non-responders in terms of various characteristics at earlier stages. This information was uniquely available to this research from some of the previous NCDS data which were linked to the results of this survey.

There were few important biases in the final sample. Those young people who responded were more likely to have a higher educational attainment and greater educational ability than the non-responders. Those who had lived in owner-occupied homes or whose fathers were in non-manual occupations when the young people were aged 16 were more likely to respond than those who lived in rented homes or whose fathers were in manual occupations. Young people who said they would like to go on to further education after leaving school were more likely to respond than those who did not want to go on to further education. The responders were more likely to have parents who showed an interest in their progress at school than the non-responders (this last variable was the only very significant bias in the sample). From the data on non-response it is reasonable to expect a *maximum* difference of 6 per cent from the true percentage, for the level of any of these variables. In other words, the results shown below are likely to under-estimate slightly the disadvantaged position of the handicapped and other groups.

Summary

The fieldwork was carried out in the summer and autumn of 1976, when the subjects were 18-year-olds. 508 interviews were completed among the four sample groups: handicapped, received special help, would benefit from it and non-handicapped. The response rate was 82 per cent at the fieldwork stage. There were few significant biases in the sample. As the four sample groups were based on different sampling fractions, with only the handicapped group consisting of the total at 16, results which follow are generally presented separately for each of these groups. This enables comparisons to be made between groups. Since the main aim of the survey was to describe some early labour market experiences of handicapped young people, in some sections analysis is carried out within the handicapped group alone or with just the non-handicapped group as a point of reference.

Most of the results which are shown later in the book are presented in terms of percentages. In tables they are generally rounded to the first decimal place and, in the text, to the nearest whole number. All the tables on which the analysis is based were tested for statistical significance and the results of such tests are quoted. The convention followed in reporting statistical significance, to demonstrate that findings are unlikely to have arisen by chance, is to use 'significant' for cases where the chi square test revealed that the associations discovered were unlikely to have arisen by chance more than 5 times in 100 ($p = < 0.05$) and 'very significant' where the chance is once in 100 ($p = < 0.01$) or once in 1000 ($p = < 0.001$). Fuller details of such tests are given in the notes at the end of the book. Unless otherwise stated the ESN(S) are omitted from the following analyses.[26]

3

Disadvantage in the Labour Market

Some case studies

There is always a danger, in any research based on the survey method, that the impact on the individual of the various processes being studied is lost. The analysis of survey data inevitably shifts attention from the individual to groups of people and to general trends.

This survey, like others, relied on the goodwill of those taking part. Sometimes the young people gave as much as 3 hours of their time. Although common causal factors and underlying influences were distinguishable, individual experiences were diverse, not only between the handicapped and non-handicapped, but often within these groups. Although depressingly some of the worst experiences were shared, all too often, by handicapped young people, there were many different individual variations. In this chapter, therefore, some of the young people (and their parents) tell their own stories of their experiences. In subsequent chapters the various points illustrated here concerning employment, unemployment, underemployment and job stability are examined in greater detail.

These examples were not randomly selected but were picked to be representative of at least some of the most common early career patterns encountered in the sample. As little editing of comments as possible has been carried out, but of course real names have not been used.

Handicapped (ESN(M) and illiterate) underemployed

Lawrence had no physical handicap, but he was formally ascertained as ESN(M) and thus attended a residential special school: 'a boarding school for people who have trouble reading and writing', as he described it. A lack of reading ability appeared to be Lawrence's main problem, and this stood between him and the realisation of his ambitions. To remedy this he was taking part in the Adult Literacy Scheme. 'I want to be better when I have to fill in forms, like at interviews.'

Another of Lawrence's ambitions had been similarly frustrated: 'I would like to go into the Army, to be a Sergeant Major, but I can't do it because of my handwriting.' At the time of the interview Lawrence had been unemployed for sixteen months, a situation which he found very distressing. Prior to this he had held three jobs, the first of which he had fixed up himself whilst still at school. The job had entailed wrapping up pieces of rubber, to be cured in a steam pan, but the powdered chalk used in the operation affected his chest and he left after two months. His brother, who worked in a store, arranged an interview for Lawrence and so he got his second job – as a shop porter. This was even more shortlived. 'I got the sack because I had two weeks off, being sick. They didn't give me a reason why.' He had seen his next job advertised at the Careers Office; it turned out to be the worst of his jobs. 'I was a shovel-maker. I just worked on two machines, cutting the corners off a shovel and punching two holes ready to put the handle in. It was boring, child's play. Anyone could do it. It was low money and very dirty, and the dirt affected my chest. The foreman was a misery as well.'

Within two months Lawrence could not tolerate the factory conditions any longer, and he left to seek a better job. He was still searching when interviewed. By then he felt that *any* job would be better than unemployment. 'If you have been out of work for, say, a year, they should have somewhere to go where you can do some sort of work. Anything would be better than being at home all the time.'

What sort of preparation for employment did Lawrence receive whilst at school? The school had a careers teacher, from whom Lawrence learnt about pay-sheets and budgeting money. He was taught about interview techniques and the importance of being polite. There were class discussions about jobs and visits to three factories. 'At one factory we saw things and they said that one part would be too noisy, and another part would be too dirty. And then at another factory it would be too quiet, it would drive us batty. It showed us some things we wouldn't like to do.'

A careers officer also visited the school. At his interview, Lawrence told the careers officer that he would like a loading-bay job, or a job with plenty of exercise. However, Lawrence had at this time already fixed up his first job during one of his weekends at home. It seemed that he saw little point talking to a careers officer in an area some distance from his home. 'The careers officer at school could have had a word with the one at home, so that I could have seen him when I came home at weekends.'

In some ways Lawrence felt that his school *had* prepared him for the responsibilities of adult life; for example: 'If we broke a window we had to pay for it, and that showed us that we couldn't go around destroying other people's property without paying for it.' In other ways the sheltered life at his residential school left him ill-prepared. 'At school you've got everything offered to you on a plate. You don't have to buy your own clothes. My biggest shock was the first time I bought a shirt and it cost me £3. My jaw nearly hit the ground!' Lawrence's income was £9.70 a week, from supplementary benefit, from which he was left £2, after contributing to his mother's housekeeping money.

His prospects of work were very gloomy. His mother commented: 'Employers in factories don't want to know you unless you can read and write; they just want their work done. If you can't read and write people look down on you and put on you. They don't give you a chance.' However Lawrence himself felt that he has done 'better than most. Some lads I know have never had a job.'

Handicapped (ESN(M)) very stable labour market history

Steven considers himself: 'luckier than most . . . I had a job straight away after leaving school. I did my training before leaving, so it wasn't too difficult to get a job.'

An account of Steven's schooling indicates why his situation is different from that of many other ESN(M) young people who find it so difficult to get stable employment. He attended a special day school for the educationally subnormal, but left the main part of the school at the age of 15 to spend his final year in an industrial training unit attached to the school. As he explained: 'We went to the training unit and they found what we did best and trained us for a job. You signed a form if you wanted to go. I decided it was a good way of training for a job, not just doing another year in class. It was all arranged by the school.'

At the unit Steven completed a course as a capstan-lathe operator Other aspects of careers work were not neglected by the school. In weekly careers lessons Steven learnt about machine-work and jobs in different factories. With the aid of films and visits to factories 'we saw what it was like and what you were supposed to do in a factory. Some people found that they didn't like it at all, so they wouldn't try to get jobs in factories.'

On leaving the training unit in July 1974 (when he was 16) Steven immediately started a job as a capstan-lathe operator − a job which he still held two years later. His training instructor at the unit had suggested he apply for the job and had sent a report to the employer. He says of his first few days at work: 'It was great, I really enjoyed going. I was pleased to be going there as I wanted to be at work. It was just great.' He is happy in his work: 'It's good money and I like the work. If I got stuck the foreman would show me. I like it there. The people are not too bossy or anything. I get on all right.' Steven meets some of his workmates outside work, although his two closest friends are childhood friends.

In addition he felt that his job was secure: 'I've been there two years now, and I seem to be getting on all right.' Steven's only complaint was of the noise, and the dirt caused by the cutting oil flying around. Steven was not without ambition. Whilst he did not wish to move from working with machines, he would like training, to extend his skills to other types of machines. Unfortunately he did not know how to find out about training courses.

Steven explained the apparent ease with which he settled into a steady job by the preparation he received at school. His advice to other young people still at school is to 'Do some training for a job before you leave, like I did.'

Handicapped (maladjusted) very unstable employment history

Peter lived with his mother who was physically disabled. He left his boarding school for maladjusted children in July 1974. He took no formal examinations, but wanted to take CSE or 'O' levels, though he doubted his own ability. But he was not given the opportunity. Why leave school then? 'When you're sixteen you leave.' Peter learnt to play the guitar at school and would have liked to learn to read music.

Looking back on school he was happy most of the time and liked it very much: 'I was enjoying it, like a superior home life. I was dreading the thought of leaving.' He felt that the school should have helped him to go on to a further education college, or night school, to get some qualifications: 'enough to get me a job as a car mechanic.' He had not taken part in any further education or training since leaving school and had not considered doing so – in fact he did not know if he would if the chance arose.

There was no specialist careers teacher at his school, but he talked in detail to one of his teachers about leaving school: 'He just told me it wouldn't be easy looking for a job. He told me what it would be like – longer hours and so on. He told me what a gaffer would be like. Prepared me for work, type of thing, put me on the right track, I hope'. Peter was very glad the teacher had given him advice. 'They threw me into it. If I said what is it like working 40 hours a week, they would tell me. They said you are knackered at first but you would get used to it. If they hadn't talked to me I'd still be figuring it out now. They told me all the bad points, like if you don't hit it off right with the manager and if you don't see the end product in the factory its a dead-end job.' But he did not get any practical help from school in finding a job.

When interviewed, Peter did not have a job. Since leaving school, in July 1974, Peter had held at least twelve jobs. The first was in a paper mill. His mother got him this job as she worked there. It lasted three months before he left because he 'didn't get on with anyone there'. He then went through a succession of jobs, all at the semi-skilled or unskilled level, for example, as a carpet cutter in a carpet warehouse, kitchen porter, labourer and barman. None of the jobs lasted longer than four months and usually considerably less. Altogether he was unemployed for some four months out of the two years.

Peter got his many jobs through the local jobcentre, his parents or by calling on the off-chance at factories or shops. He was disillusioned with private employment agencies (considering them a 'waste of bus fares') but got a lot of help from his local jobcentre. 'They helped me a lot. They got me jobs straight away, just like that, without any messing around. They gave me six and said "which one suits you best?"'

His last job was as a kitchen porter which entailed washing pots and pans and mopping floors. A typical day? 'Get screamed at, use the dish-washing machine and mop the floors – that's it.' It took him over an hour to get there; he was standing all day and earned £24 a week, gross. He didn't think of the job as permanent when he was doing it. 'At that time I was on emergency tax, which was a silly idea. I got more off the dole. My bus fares to work – that took a lump out of it as well. Just washing dishes wasn't exciting . . . I knew I wouldn't be in it for long; it's for old fellows, just like a lollipop man's job.' In fact he disliked this job very much and took it only because there were no others available. It was 'absolutely miserable. I disliked everything. It was greasy; I had to wash my hair everyday.'

What did he remember about his first few days at work? 'The first thing I remember, which I'll never forget, is being sent for a long stand. They said "just stand there" – I'll never forget it. Also there was the feeling of independence. I felt "great, I can look after myself". I remember when that feeling had dwindled – the feeling of the replacement of old school friends by new friends and teachers by gaffers.' The most important aspect of work for him was having friendly people at work with him 'because if they are horrible it ruins your work'. Next he wanted to take a pride in his work, 'because if you don't have pride in it you don't do it half as good'.

Peter's mother was disabled and not working at the time of the interview. She was not happy with the school that he had attended, 'because I felt the school had a couldn't-care-less attitude towards the boys. They were allowed to do more or less what they liked as long as they didn't get up to too much mischief, and because of this, when he came here he didn't know how to behave in a home or how to treat it, it was just like a playground. I don't think they helped there really enough as regards careers and education.'

His mother also felt that he should have been helped to take some examinations, 'sufficient exams to have been able to get the career he wanted and I would have liked him to learn music properly.' She was equally unhappy with the advice Peter received at school about jobs: 'I don't think they were told nearly enough and what they told them weren't important things. They seem to concentrate on factory jobs, assume all are going into factories which they weren't. They weren't shown enough variety in jobs, to me they could have taken a more personal interest in what the boys were actually interested in. It's not as if it was a big school with a lot of boys in.'

She also felt that employers had little understanding of Peter's kind of handicap: 'Well, the majority of employers are slave drivers. They want as much work out of you as quickly as possible and they are not prepared to let you learn, they expect you to pick up a job in five minutes, whereas if they give you the time to learn, then you could be really good at the job.'

Handicapped (partially-sighted) stable employment history

The most important ingredient for a happy job is 'being equal with workmates'. This was Sharon's opinion. Her life over the last few years had been a fight to overcome failing sight and to gain a secure position — a position of independence. Besides being partially sighted Sharon also has a disability which causes her joints to come out of their sockets. However it was the deterioration of her sight which was of most concern to Sharon, and which contributed to her decision to leave school at 16.

She attended a special residential school for the partially sighted, where she took seven CSE's (and passed one at grade one), but she decided to leave to get established in a job, and thus become independent, before her eyesight failed completely. Independence was very important to Sharon, partly because of the attitude of her father. 'My father had kept me for 16 years and he didn't see why he should do so any longer. He wanted me to go out to work.' The tension in her home life was such that she said: 'I was happy at school *because* I was away from home — it's not a very happy family.' However whilst she was sorry to have left the friends she made at school, she felt glad to have achieved some measure of independence.

On the whole Sharon felt that the advice and support she received at school was inadequate. 'The teachers could have tried to place themselves in the position of the partially sighted, instead of just saying "no, you can't do that, because of your eyesight." It would have been better if some of the teachers had been partially sighted, to have understood better.' This was particularly true with regard to careers advice, but also in other matters Sharon felt a need 'to talk to teachers more often about problems. You tended to keep them to yourself . . . An older person's advice would have been more help'.

Sharon appeared to have received no formal instruction about employment at her school, with the exception of one visit to a catering college. The visit was at the suggestion of a careers officer in response to Sharon's declared interest in catering. This was the same careers officer who visited the school. However, the careers officer whom Sharon visited in her home town had different views and told her she would be a hazard in the kitchen. Her interests in child care were dismissed 'because I wouldn't cope with the training, for example, thermometers, or if a child had something in its mouth I may not see it'. She was also deemed unsuitable for the Armed Forces, because of her sight.

So Sharon received no constructive advice with regard to the careers which interested her, and she was most dissatisfied. 'The careers officer went through all the jobs that might be suitable and decided I was only fit to fill shelves in a supermarket.' Later she visited a jobcentre but with no success. Private agencies were more fruitful − 'until they found out about my eyesight.'

Sharon's first three jobs − temporary relief work during the summer after she left school − were all found through a private employment agency. She worked for a printer first and then as a typist. However, the best and most interesting job she ever had was a temporary job as a computer data-processing clerk: 'I was able to stand my ground with everyone else.'

At the time of the interview Sharon worked as an office junior, a job which she had held eighteen months. Her duties included some typing, working a switchboard, acting as receptionist and messenger, and making the tea. However she felt insecure in the job 'because I'm getting a bit old to be an office junior', and yet there were no prospects of a better job within the firm. As for the future: 'In three years' time I'll be lucky if I'm in work at all, with gradually losing my eyesight.' A further factor, contributing to her general unhappiness at work was her feeling of inferiority: 'The other girls make me feel inferior to them. There are only three days between my age and that of the typist. But in a way I'm babyfied.'

Sharon found the job through a newspaper advertisement, and took it because it was the only one she was offered. Seven or more interviews for other jobs had all been unsuccessful, usually because of her sight or her lack of training. Her mother felt that employers did not want to take the risk of employing someone with partial sight because 'they know nothing about it. They are frightened'. Sharon would like to train as a telephonist − 'my last resort'. In the meantime her advice to a younger partially sighted person about to leave school was 'to try to prove everybody wrong'.

Handicapped (physically) underemployed

Elaine had a congenital heart condition, and had had major heart surgery when an artificial valve was inserted. She was appreciably physically, but not mentally, handicapped and lived with her parents. Elaine attended an ordinary comprehensive school. She missed about seven months through ill-health but caught up 'very quickly'. She was unemployed when interviewed and had only had one job since leaving school in July 1974.

She did not need any special help in school, but did not take any examinations. Why leave? She was not very happy at school. 'I didn't like it, the atmosphere, the cattiness of the girls.' Her parents did not mind her leaving at 16. 'She wanted to leave and we wanted her to be happy.' Elaine was not nervous at the thought of leaving school; on the contrary she was glad to get away because of her unfortunate experience. Looking back she was 'glad to get away from the bad atmosphere'.

Elaine wanted to do a further education course in art or design – she was principally interested in art work. She talked with her mother and father about further education, but they 'realise I can't cope with travelling to and from school or college because of my heart condition'. This she felt was preventing her from taking a course.

There was a careers teacher at her last school and Elaine saw her several times. The careers teacher was very helpful, and a relief in an unhappy school life. 'She was someone to turn to. She gave me some ideas about what it was like outside school.' In careers lessons they also talked about work and different jobs such as the Police and RAF', but they were not suitable for Elaine. Elaine had heard about careers officers but she had not talked to one. However she did see a disablement resettlement officer (DRO) and, in fact, got her only job through him. She felt school should have helped her to mix more: 'more group discussion, to get to know people better, teachers and pupils. Mix the children more when they come from different schools'.

Elaine had held only one job since leaving school. This was a post as a junior clerk which the DRO obtained for her as soon as she left school. The job consisted of typing and filing. People were friendly and helpful at work and she enjoyed it very much, but after a few months she was taken ill and was dismissed 'without them really finding out about my illness'. The main barrier to getting another job was her inability to travel to and from work. Ideally she would like a job as a receptionist or in clerical work. The most important aspects of work for her were friendly workmates and being able to take a pride in her work.

Elaine tried to make the best of the fact that she was not working. 'I have time to do things like painting, cooking and crocheting.' Her mother wanted her to take 'O' levels, 'but ill-health prevented her. I wouldn't force her in any way'. She was happy with the advice Elaine received at school but was unhappy about the help given to young people like Elaine, especially in employment. There should be a 'change of attitudes by employers. They don't want the responsibility. They don't have any consideration. There are so many unemployed they want five 'O' levels to lick stamps'.

Handicapped (ESN(M)) fully employed

'When my Dad left home it hit me. I could not get on at school and everything was upset. That put me off learning and concentrating at school. I was always playing truant. The teachers did not bother with me and let me do as I wanted. I did not do a stroke of work. I got in with a bad set, got into trouble with the police, and ran away from home. I was put on probation. I knew then it was too late to catch up on school work and I got to the state where I just did not care . . . I regret now that I wasted the time.'

This is how Rosalind remembered her last years at school. Although previously ascertained as educationally subnormal, Rosalind was attending an ordinary school by this time, and receiving extra help in reading and arithmetic. Hence she has been included in the group of ESN(M) young people. She took two CSEs, but never returned to school to find out whether she had passed. She left school at age 16 because 'all I wanted was to work in a hairdresser's.'.

Rosalind's ambitions had been achieved, and the change in her had been considerable. What were the means by which this change occurred? The school certainly did provide some formal career instruction and Rosalind remembered some of the lessons. 'The teacher talked about different jobs and handed out booklets, but I was not interested.' However, because of her frequent absences from school, Rosalind did not benefit from attending many lessons. She did attend an interview with a careers officer, accompanied by her mother, during which hairdressing was discussed, but by this time a job had been fixed up anyway. It was Rosalind's mother who encouraged her and helped Rosalind for the most part. 'She asked my present employer if he would take me on.' This was whilst Rosalind was still at school and she began working at the hairdressers every Saturday, some evenings and during her holidays. It was later arranged that she would stay with this employer full-time when she left school. 'My boss was very confident in me. He could see I wanted to get on and that one day I would be a good hairdresser. He gave me confidence and that made me realise that there was something I could do . . . especially after being so hopeless at school. He is a very understanding boss.'

Two years later Rosalind had nearly finished her apprenticeship as a hairdresser: 'I now do cuts, perms, colours, sets, everything. I have between six and thirteen clients a day'. Her training had involved one evening class a week in the salon, working on models. Remembering her first day at work she said 'My feet were killing me, but I seemed to get on well with the clients and staff'. She said of the other staff, 'We are very close and feel free to talk about things.' Although she felt that her wages (£15 a week take-home pay) were too low, she was happy in the job. 'I wanted to use my hands and do something artistic. I've never wanted to do anything else.'

Would have benefited from special help, very unstable employment history

Christopher had been working for nearly one year when he was interviewed. He had no health problems, and lived with his parents and three younger brothers and sisters. He had been given special help with reading and spelling at his secondary modern school. Before leaving in July 1974 he took three CSEs — physics, history and mathematics — but did not pass any at grade one. He had also wanted to take geography. 'The teacher seemed to think I was not good enough. I think it was my spelling that held me back.' He also wanted more coaching in maths. Why leave school? 'Because I wanted to get a job. I did not think I would get any further at school.' His parents left the decision to him. 'They said it was up to me, it was my decision. If I could not get any further I must do what was right for me.' Christopher was happy in school. He was never bored or fed up with the teachers and was nervous at the thought of leaving. 'At times I would like to be back at school but when it comes to finance and evenings out, I am glad I am at work.'

The careers teacher at Christopher's school found him his first job, as an assistant storekeeper. He also talked to other teachers about careers. 'I took it all and thought it over − there was a laboratory technician's job going at school, but the headmaster thought there was too little gap between me and the fifth year students.' Christopher talked to the careers officer when he came to the school and mentioned the laboratory technician's job. The careers officer agreed that this was suitable but the headmaster did not agree. He did not think the interview was very helpful: 'Somehow things came to a standstill − nothing came from the interview'. He also spoke to the science teacher about careers. 'He seemed to think the laboratory technician job was a good idea, but when I got the stores job he thought that was all right.' There were no careers lessons at Christopher's school, but he did take part in work experience − a three-day release period in stores-work. 'It gave me an insight into the job.' Could his school have done more? 'It was the best they could do − there were so many other kids wanting jobs.'

Christopher had held four jobs since leaving school. He was a service mechanic at the time of the interview. This entailed 'starting at 8 a.m. I get through a few fittings in the morning, which is a five-hour stretch, and fill out reports on the fittings as they come in. In the afternoon I get through another two fittings.' He had no training for the job, being shown what to do in three days. He got the job through the labour exchange. Christopher was not sure how permanent this job was: 'as far as I want it to be. I might change my mind tomorrow and want another job.' He got on well with the people at work and was happy in the job. 'It is nice because you are free to decide your own action regarding the work.' Christopher said he would like to do a full-time further education course in engineering or photography, or a part-time course if his firm would let him.

When he left school he had gone straight to the job as a store keeper, where he stayed for five months. This was the worst job he did. 'I was a bit green out of school and was put on.' He was then offered a job as a sprayer in the same firm. He was in this job for six months. 'It just got too much, the noise from the big oven by the side of me got me down.' Christopher got another job immediately, as a grass cutter. This lasted two months. 'I had transport but was only a learner-driver. My co-driver got the sack, so I could not get there.' He was then unemployed for ten weeks before he got his latest job. What did Christopher remember about his first few days at work? 'They didn't go too bad. It felt a bit strange with the new machines and I had to get used to the form filling.' The most important aspect of a job for him is friendly people with whom to work. His ideal job would be in the Army, in the tank corps. Looking back on his two years in the labour market Christopher said: 'I have had a fair bit of luck and experience'. Advice to a younger person leaving school? 'Don't take any nonsense from anyone but the governor or fore-man, and remember you have certain rights.'

Non-handicapped, very stable employment history

Ever since he was five years old Gerald had wanted to be a farmer. So it was that when he reached seventeen he was eager to leave school. 'I wanted to get away, to get on the ground. I'd rather be outside than stuck inside all day.' Already for two years Gerald had been working on a farm at weekends, and he had discussed his choice of career with the farmer and his parents had also talked to the adviser to the Agricultural Training Board. Gerald was particu-larly grateful to his careers officer since it was from him that he had heard details of the agricultural college which he attended. The careers teacher at his school had also talked to him about this possi-bility. When Gerald left his secondary school, having taken seven CSEs, he embarked on a nine-month introductory course at the agricultural college. After this he became an apprentice with his present employer and had been attending the college on day release. When he completes the course he hopes to be a machine craftsman.

Gerald's work involved 'planting crops, dealing with irrigation pipes and general jobs on the farm'. He admitted that there is not the variety in the work which he had expected ('Everybody seems to specialise') and he disliked the cold and wet, and the very long hours, but on the whole he was happy. He had a 'useful' job, in the open, with friendly helpful workmates. He hoped one day to have his own farm. So with support and informed advice Gerald was on the way to achieving his life-long ambition, even though this had meant giving up some things. 'With a job like I've got on a farm you don't see your friends so much. That's partly my fault − I don't go out in the evenings.' However, 'I think I've come further in life than a lot of students have. They are still at college full-time and still doing theory. I've done theory and practical, *and* earned a wage.'

4
Young People and the Labour Market

In this chapter I describe the kinds of jobs that the young people obtained on entering the labour market, and their experience of unemployment and I begin to outline the disadvantages suffered by handicapped young people. But first it is necessary to refer briefly to official and other data on school-leaving and employment, in order to demonstrate the general setting within which their transition from school to work took place.

Factors influencing the employment of young people

The overall employment position of school-leavers and other young people depends on a number of interrelated factors: for example, the level of aggregate demand (whether created by central planning or market forces) and thus employment in the economy as a whole and the number of opportunities for young people, that is, the demands of employers. These in turn, depend to a great extent on the structure of, and level of technology in, different industries. Employers' perceptions of the productivity and relative costs of young workers compared to older workers are also influential. In addition, institutional factors, including retirement and recruitment policies, can contribute to the demand for young workers.

On the other side there are 'supply factors', including the size of the group in question and the number seeking employment, as opposed to further or higher education. Supply factors, particularly individual and personal characteristics, have tended to dominate some explanations and popular conceptions of the causes of unemployment.[1] For example, some unemployment is said to result from high levels of welfare benefits and the free choice of the unemployed to remain so.[2] More often unemployment is explained in terms of the characteristics of the unemployed themselves: age, sex, health, ethnic origin and so on. The problem with this sort of description is that unemployment is seen as being endemically linked to certain personal characteristics. Some economists go so far as to argue that about 30 per cent of the unemployed should be excluded from the unemployment register, because they are poor unemployment prospects.[3] Clearly personal characteristics short of extremely severe disability, do not, in themselves make an individual unemployable. Rather they are a key factor in determining the employability of a person in a particular labour market situation and within a particular form of industrial organisation. Employability is determined by the level of overall demand and its local variations, and by the interactions of personal characteristics with employment policies, employer preferences and choices. One indication of the importance of demand factors in creating unemployment is the ratio of unemployed people to vacancies, which is currently (1981) more than ten to one.[4]

Having established the need to examine both demand and supply factors in the labour market, it is important to note two further assumptions underlying the subsequent analysis. Few of the factors under consideration are historically stable; the occupational structure and the size and quality of the workforce have changed considerably in the last century and can be expected to continue to do so. Less obvious, secondly, is the need to assess employment and employability relatively and over time. Disproportionately high levels of unemployment among unskilled workers must be related to job status and security of tenure in other parts of the labour force. Thus jobs rather than people may be compared according to their attributes: status, security, hours, working conditions, pay, fringe benefits and so on, and therefore their effects on the incumbents. Some categories of jobs may be expanded or contracted in line with demand, as a result of a change in investment policy, or as a normally accepted seasonal change. Thus some workers, particularly the unskilled, may experience occasional spells out of work, and perhaps accept them as a normal feature of their working life.[5] This implies that the dichotomy between employment and unemployment is too simple and falsely represents the true nature of employment experience. There is, in fact, a continuum of labour market experiences, stretching from secure employment, through interrupted employment to continuous unemployment.[6]

The research reported here was carried out against a backcloth of high and rising unemployment in the labour force as a whole. In September 1973 there was a total of 526 900 registered as unemployed in Great Britain; in September 1975, 1 096 900 and in September 1977, 1 541 800, an increase of over one million. By September 1980 this had increased by a further 500 000.[7] This has been accompanied by a growing concern about the deterioration of job prospects for young people, a concern reflected in the emergency job creation measures initiated in 1975. The main reason for this is the large increase in the number of unemployed young people since 1973. In September 1973 there were 13 000 school-leavers registered as unemployed; by September 1980 there were over 200 000.

According to the Manpower Services Commission: 'Past changes in occupational structure are unlikely to be reversed'.[8] It is expected that the demand for unskilled and unqualified workers will continue to decline. Also as a result of the 'de-skilling' of some occupations, the demand for traditional craft skills learnt in apprenticeship is likely to decline. At the same time the demand for workers in clerical, sales and service occupations is expected to remain fairly stable. Even the most optimistic projections of future employment indicate that the levels of unemployment among young people will continue to remain very high.[9]

Into work – type and status of employment

Future prospects for the employment of school-leavers and young people are poor, at least in the short run. On the evidence of past experience, whatever happens to the overall level of employment, handicapped young people will remain at a considerable disadvantage compared to the non-handicapped, as indicated, for example, by their disproportionate share of long-term unemployment. Having looked briefly at the overall situation for young people, we now turn to an analysis of the employment status of the sample of 18-year-olds.

At the time of interview three-fifths of the sample were in paid employment, one-fifth were unemployed and just over one-tenth were still at school. But as could be expected from the preceding discussion, the experiences of different groups within the sample were quite different. Table 4.1 shows the current employment status for each of the four sample groups.

What is immediately striking about this table is the high rate of unemployment amongst all groups, *except* for the non-handicapped. This particularly applied to the handicapped group, where at least one in four had no job. Analysis of young people with different types of handicap reveals that unemployment was particularly high among the maladjusted where one-third were out of work. Although many of those in adult training centres or sheltered workshops were classified as severely educationally subnormal, more than one-third were not so classified. The comparatively low numbers of non-handicapped people in work is more than offset by the numbers still in school, two-thirds of whom said they had jobs to go to when they left. Differences between the employment status of the handicapped and non-handicapped shown in Table 4.1 were statistically very significant.

TABLE 4.1 *Employment status at the time of interview (%)*

Current employment status	Handi-capped[c]	Special help	Would benefit	Non-handicapped
Employed[a]	47.8	78.3	72.2	66.4
Unemployed				
seeking work	19.1	13.0	20.4	4.4
not seeking work	8.0	4.4	1.9	—
Still at school or in further education	5.6	4.4	5.6	29.2
Adult training centre or sheltered workshop	14.7	—	—	—
Other[b]	4.8	—	—	—
Total	100	100	100	100
Number	251	69	54	113

Handicapped *vs* non-handicapped: $X^2 = 82.75$, 4 degrees of freedom, $p < 0.001$
[a] Includes one working unpaid
[b] Includes hospital, borstal
[c] Includes the ESN(S)

Type of work

What kinds of work did the young people do? On a national basis, about one-third of young people in work are doing manufacturing jobs and about one-fifth distribution and transport work, and there are significant differences between the sexes in some occupations such as distribution and construction.[10]

In this survey, type of work was classified according to eight main categories, with ninety-eight sub-groups. The system was the same as that used in the most recent NCDS follow-up, in order to facilitate comparisons with previous data. These are the primary groups together with examples of constituent jobs:

Farming, forestry and fishing	farmer, farm-worker, game-keeper, gardener
Artistic, creative and sporting	creative artist, designer, journalist, model, sportsman, disc jockey
Professional, managerial, technical	teacher, researcher, solicitor, doctor, pilot, nurse, social worker, administrator, priest, draughtsman
Service workers	policeman, fireman, postman, driver, salesman, caterer, hairdresser, shop assistant
Clerical and office work	secretary, clerk, cashier, office machine operator
Manual work (industrial)	plumber, bricklayer, painter, mechanic, fitter, welder, carpenter, storekeeper, labourer, miner
Armed forces, merchant navy	
Craftsmen	butcher, tailor, cobbler, jeweller

Commenting on the industrial distribution of young people in 1964, Carter noted the predominance of manufacturing industry.[11] That position was confirmed 12 years later by this survey of 18-year-olds, with 48 per cent of those who were in open employment working in industrial manufacturing jobs. (These and other percentages in this section refer only to those young people who have held a job since leaving school. Those still at school, in further education, adult training centres, or continuously unemployed are excluded.) In the majority of the tables below using the variable 'type of work', construction and engineering are combined with other forms of industrial work.

A closer look at the types of work done revealed some important variations between the groups, for example in clerical and manual-industrial employment (see Table 6.1). However, within this latter type of employment, the non-handicapped were nearly three times as likely as the handicapped to have jobs in engineering trades. The handicapped were more likely to work as, for example, packers, warehousemen and labourers, while the non-handicapped more often got engineering apprenticeships. Isolating the ESN(M) group, it was found that as many as 65 per cent had industrial jobs (including engineering and construction work). One in five of the non-handicapped group held clerical jobs, compared to only one in twenty amongst the handicapped. Furthermore, two thirds of this latter proportion consisted of physically handicapped people, so that in all, only one per cent of the ESN(M) group got clerical jobs.[12]

Level of skill and social class

For most people the quality of their experience of work, and much of the rest of life, depends on the type of work they do. Of particular importance is the *form* of work, that is, whether it is a manual or non-manual task and what degree of skill it requires. These factors contribute to the status, or social standing, that are ascribed to different jobs and people in society. So there is a hierarchy of occupational groups and numerous studies have shown that these groupings are good predictors of many other factors including income, education, attitudes and interests, which taken together form the concept of social class.[13]

The concept of social class is used extensively in this research, so a brief explanation is called for. It is assumed that *social class is a grouping of people into categories on the basis of occupation*.[14] Despite recent criticism of the scale, the best known and most widely used classification is used: the Registrar General's social class categorisation, derived from the *Classification of Occupations*, 1970.[15] This lists over 20 000 separate occupational titles, which in turn are grouped into 200 occupational units, each having a social class classification.

There are five separate social classes in the Registrar-General's classification: professional, intermediate, skilled, partly skilled and unskilled. In practice social class III (skilled) is usually split into non-manual and manual and often class IV (semi-skilled) is similarly divided. The following are examples of occupations included in each class:

I	*Professional*	accountant, doctor, lawyer
II	*Intermediate*	farmer, manager, schoolteacher, engineer
III	*Skilled non-manual*	secretary, shop assistant, waiter, clerical worker, sales representative
III	*Skilled manual*	bus driver, bricklayer, carpenter, cook, electrician, butcher
IV	*Partly skilled*	agricultural worker, bus conductor, packer, postman, telephone operator
V	*Unskilled*	kitchen hand, labourer, lorry driver's mate, messenger, office cleaner, window cleaner

Table 4.2 showing the social class distribution of the young people in the sample, illustrates the very wide differences in occupational status between the handicapped and non-handicapped.

Table 4.2 includes a column showing the social class distribution of all economically active 15–24-year-olds in the 1971 Census. However, this provides only a rough yardstick because of the difference in age groups. The difference between the four sample groups in skilled non-manual, skilled manual, semi-skilled or unskilled work was statistically very significant. There was obviously a close relationship between social class and type of work, but one which differed between the two main sample groups. For example, taking the handicapped first, all those in the skilled non-manual occupational class were working either in the service or clerical sectors, 62 per cent in the former, and 38 per cent in the latter.[16] Among the non-handicapped nearly 75 per cent of the skilled non-manual were in clerical jobs and the remainder in service and professional jobs. Turning to the skilled manual class, only 16 per cent of the handicapped in this class were in service sector jobs, while 20 per cent were in engineering and 40 per cent in industrial manual work. By

TABLE 4.2 *Social class of first jobs (%)*

Social class[b]	Sample group				
	Handi capped[c]	Special help	Would benefit	Non-handi- capped	All 15–24- year-olds
Professional and Intermediate	0.0	1.6	0.0	9.9	14
Skilled					
non-manual	11.8	21.8	21.6	33.3	15
manual[d]	24.1	15.6	35.3	32.1	44
Semi-skilled					
non-manual	4.1	3.1	0.0	3.7	17
Semi-skilled					
manual	37.6	48.4	31.4	14.8	
Unskilled	22.3	9.4	11.8	6.2	9
Total	100	100	100	100	100
Number	170	64	51	81	

$X^2 = 43.5$, 9 degrees of freedom, $p < 0.001$
[a] Includes only those who have worked. Based on first job.
[b] Excludes those whose jobs were unclassifiable.
[c] Excludes ESN(S).
[d] Includes the Armed Services.

comparison, nearly 50 per cent of the skilled manual non-handicapped young people had engineering jobs.

These important differences in occupational class and type of work underlie much of the subsequent analysis. The majority of the handicapped were working in industrial manual employment. However the marked differences within occupational classes between the type of work done by handicapped and non-handicapped were less predictable. In addition to those noted above, 50 per cent of the handicapped in semi-skilled jobs were in the industrial manual sector, compared with 36 per cent of the non-handicapped, whilst 12 per cent of the handicapped and 28 per cent of the non-handicapped were in farming jobs.

Sex differences

Social class differences were influenced by the significant sexual divisions in occupation to which I referred earlier (p. 40). Young men were more likely to go into manual occupations and women into non-manual jobs. But what was the situation amongst handicapped young people? A significantly higher proportion of handicapped men than women went into unskilled work (26 per cent compared with 12 per cent). A slightly lower proportion of men than women went into semi-skilled jobs (34 per cent compared with 37 per cent). Taking the largest group of handicapped young people – the ESN(M) – just over 66 per cent of the first jobs taken by young men were semi-skilled manual or unskilled jobs. This compares with 28 per cent of non-handicapped young men. The proportion of ESN(M) women getting jobs in the lowest social classes was 55 per cent.

For both sexes the difference between the ESN(M) and the non-handicapped was striking: seven out of ten of the former compared with two out of ten of the latter obtained semi-skilled manual or unskilled first jobs. Half of the non-handicapped young men who had worked since leaving school started in skilled manual jobs, and just over half of the girls started in skilled non-manual jobs. One in two men who had received special help in ordinary schools went into semi-skilled manual occupations, while the same proportion of those who would have benefited from such help went into skilled manual jobs.

So, on the basis of information about the social class of the school-leavers' *first* jobs, significant differences began to emerge between the handicapped and non-handicapped in terms of occupational status. The majority of the former entered low skill, low status jobs, while the bulk of the latter obtained skilled or even higher status employment. No account is taken here of the greater tendency for the non-handicapped to remain in full-time further education.

Turning now to the social class distribution of the young person's *current and latest* job: a similarly high proportion (61 per cent) of handicapped young people were in semi-skilled and unskilled manual jobs, while the percentage for the non-handicapped was 18.[17] The ratio between handicapped and non-handicapped at the other end of the class scale was even wider, with the latter having over four times the proportion of the former in the top three classes (skilled non-manual, intermediate and professional). There was in fact very little sign of an *overall* shift in the class composition between first and current (or latest) jobs. This may disguise several notable success stories and some failures, but the average picture remained fairly constant. Of course two years in work is too short a period to expect any major shifts in occupational status.

Unemployment

There are two important aspects to be considered when assessing the impact of unemployment on any group of people: *frequency* – the number of separate periods out of work; and *duration* – the length of time out of work. Table 4.3 shows that there were very significant differences between the four sample groups in their share of unemployment, as measured first by the number of periods of unemployment. Twice the proportion of the handicapped who had entered the labour market had experienced some unemployment, compared with the non-handicapped.

TABLE 4.3 *Number of periods of unemployment (%)*

	Sample group			
Number of periods unemployed	Handi-capped	Special help	Would benefit	Non-handi-capped
0	35.6	50.8	41.2	69.2
1	29.9	28.6	35.3	21.8
2	18.4	9.5	9.8	2.6
3 or more	16.1	11.1	13.7	6.4
Total	100	100	100	100
Number	174	63	51	78

$X^2 = 31.9$, 9 degrees of freedom, $p < 0.001$.

Handicapped young people also had the greatest share of unemployment in terms of duration, with nearly 33 per cent having been out of work for six months or more in two years, compared with 3 per cent of non-handicapped young people who had entered the labour market (excluding those in school or on further education or training courses).[17] Most of the non-handicapped who had been unemployed were out of work for very short periods, usually immediately after leaving school, often as a 'holiday' before starting work. Fifty per cent of the handicapped and just under 75 per cent of the non-handicapped had been continuously employed. Differences between the handicapped and non-handicapped in the length of time they were unemployed were statistically very significant.[19]

The type of work undertaken not only proves of crucial importance in determining the young people's experience of employment, but also of *un*employment. Fifty per cent of the handicapped whose latest job was in the service sector were continuously employed; 16 per cent had been unemployed for more than 12 months. In the building industry, only 25 per cent had been continuously employed and 50 per cent unemployed for three months or more; 50 per cent of the handicapped in manual industrial jobs were employed for the whole period, but 40 per cent were unemployed for three months or more and 22 per cent for one year or more. By contrast, 75 per cent of those in engineering work had been continuously employed and none had been unemployed for over six months.

Summary

This brief description of the outcome of the transition from school to work of the sample of 18-year-olds is intended to prepare the ground for the more detailed subsequent analysis. Already, though, there are clear indications of a gulf between the two main sample groups in respect of the quality and quantity of their labour market achievements. The handicapped were most disadvantaged – they were more likely to be unemployed and when they had jobs, they were usually in the lowest social classes. Although the first two years in the labour market is too short a period to examine social mobility it was immediately apparent that whatever their subsequent employment achievements, large sections of the two main sample groups had entered the labour market at different points in the occupational hierarchy – a fact that was likely to have a significant bearing on their future employment prospects and indeed, on their life chances.

5

The Working Environment

In this chapter some of the objective conditions that the young people encountered on entering work are described and some of their reactions to these conditions are considered.

The work situation represents one of the most important influences on an individual's attitude and identity. As David Lockwood has pointed out, different conditions experienced at work shape and pattern different social relationships:

> For every employee is precipitated, by virtue of a given division of labour, into unavoidable relationships with other employees, superiors, managers or customers. The work situation involves the separation and concentration of individuals, affords possibilities for identification with, and alienation from others, and conditions feelings of isolation, antagonism and solidarity.[1]

Alienation and other reactions to work are related to type of occupation and job status. The job status of young people is in general low. It was demonstrated in Chapter 4 that the job status of handicapped young people in this sample was much lower than the non-handicapped. Carter saw the low status of the jobs entered by most of the secondary modern school-leavers he studied as a perpetuation of their lowly position at school: 'insignificance at school is but a preface to insignificance at work'.[2]

There are two interrelated factors that must be distinguished in this analysis of the 18-year-olds' experience of work: the objective conditions of their working environment and their attitudes towards work. As the International Labour Organisation points out: 'A young person's first contact with working life and working conditions, and his success or failure in adapting himself to it, will often determine his attitude to work.'[3] It is the work situation which is predominant in shaping the young persons' images of the world and their place in that world.[4]

Working conditions

There were considerable differences in social class composition between the handicapped and non-handicapped young people. Was this reflected in the different conditions the young experience at work? In order to assess whether there were significant differences between the sample groups in their day-to-day experiences of working life several questions were asked about different attributes of employment such as the hours worked, and about the presence of employment facilities, like toilets and canteens.

Travel to work and hours worked

In our sample of 18-year-olds, 40 per cent of the handicapped took less than 15 minutes to get to work, compared with 37 per cent of the non-handicapped.[5] Seventy-two per cent of the non-handicapped took less than 30 minutes to get to work. This accorded with Maizels's finding, from her study of 300 under-18-year olds in Willesden, that three-quarters took no longer than 30 minutes.[6] She noted that this proportion was considerably higher than Liepmann's previous study of the journey to work.[7] Much of the difference must be explained by the lapse of 25 years between the two studies and the increased availability of personal transport such as motorcycles over that time. In fact the non-handicapped in this study were more likely to be travelling longer distances to work (measured in terms of time taken) with 28 per cent taking more than thirty minutes to get to work, compared with 17 per cent of the handicapped. This difference is underpinned by the greater representation of non-manual employment amongst the non-handicapped, which was reported in the previous chapter.

It is primarily the differences between the occupational classes of the sample groups that underlie the tendency, shown in Table 5.1, for the handicapped to work longer hours than the non-handicapped. There was also a strong tendency for the handicapped to work less than thirty hours a week. In other words, they were less likely than the non-handicapped to have 'normal' working hours. This difference was statistically very significant.

TABLE 5.1   *Number of hours worked (%)*

| Hours worked | Sample group | | | |
	Handi-capped	Special help	Would benefit	Non-handi-capped
Less than 30	5.5	0.0	2.0	0.0
30–39	18.3	19.0	19.6	35.0
40–49	68.3	71.4	66.7	57.5
50 or more	7.3	9.5	11.8	7.5
Total	100	100	100	100
Number	180	63	51	80

Handicapped *vs* non-handicapped $X^2 = 12.01$, 3 degrees of freedom, $p < 0.01$.

Three-quarters of the ESN(M) young people worked between forty and forty-nine hours a week. The majority of the 23 ESN(S) young people who were in adult training centres worked between 30 and 39 hours a week.[8]

Strenuous work

Young people were asked whether they did any heavy lifting and roughly how much time they spent doing this, for example, during the day before the interview. The handicapped were more likely to be doing heavy lifting than the non-handicapped. One half compared with over two-thirds did very little or none. In addition, the former were one-and-a-half times as likely as the latter to be spending half or more than half their time at work doing heavy lifting. Less than half the special help group did very little or no lifting and about one-seventh spent nearly all their time doing this. For the would benefit group the proportions were three-fifths and one-fifth.[9].

Work facilities

Respondents in work, and those who had worked since leaving school, were asked whether their employer provided a number of facilities commonly expected at work. These included tea or coffee (whether free or not), indoor toilets, washing facilities, indoor place to eat sandwiches, first-aid box and facility, and meal vouchers or meals.[10] A 'work facilities index' was constructed by awarding one point for each of the twelve facilities the young person named. Table 5.2 shows that the handicapped were more likely than the non-handicapped to work in poor conditions and even less likely to be working for an employer who provided all or nearly all the facilities on our index. The result was statistically very significant.

TABLE 5.2   *Facilities at places of employment (%)*

| Number of facilities | Sample group | | | |
	Handi-capped	Special help	Would benefit	Non-handi-capped
1–5	25.3	19.0	14.0	10.1
6–7	42.2	49.2	46.0	26.2
8–9	28.3	30.1	38.0	46.8
10 or more	4.2	1.6	2.0	16.4
Total	100	100	100	100
Number	166	63	50	79

Work facilities grouped 1–3, 4–5, 6–7, 8–9, 10–12 for 4 sample groups; $X^2 = 34.0$, 12 degrees of freedom, $p < 0.001$.
Handicapped *vs* non-handicapped; facilities grouped as in table; $X^2 = 20.75$, 3 degrees of freedom, $p < 0.001$.

Underlying these differences in working conditions were differences between social classes. For example, one in twelve of handicapped young people in the skilled non-manual class were in jobs with fewer than six facilities and one in six with ten or more. In contrast, one in four of the unskilled had fewer than six facilities and none of them had ten or more facilities. Dividing the handicapped into manual and non-manual workers: 96 per cent of those in jobs with fewer than six facilities were manual workers. A similar division amongst the non-handicapped revealed that 71 per cent of those working in poor conditions (1–5 facilities) were manual workers.[11]

Contact with other people at work

One of the main differences between school and work for many young people may be the degree of personal contact. Moving from a social system where many experiences are shared to one where, for example, long periods may be spent alone, or where interaction and exchange may be discouraged in the interests of production must present special difficulties. If such a work situation is encountered it may, at best, encourage alienation and privatisation.[12] There is evidence to suggest that young people place great importance on social factors associated with the work setting. In Maizels's study the highest score in a list of preferred job characteristics, on average, applied to social factors. 'The majority of young workers – nearly 66 per cent – felt that they worked with a 'good crowd' and this was the only item to receive such a high rating.'[13] A study carried out by the National Institute for Industrial Psychology found 56 per cent of young workers cited this characteristic.[14]

Young people were asked if they worked alone – only two did so. The remainder were asked whether they spoke to the people they worked with during the day; secondly whether any of these helped them with their work and thirdly, whether they saw any of them outside work. A score was constructed on the basis of their answers to the three questions to indicate the degree of contact with workmates. Only 4 per cent of the handicapped and 1 per cent of the non-handicapped had no such contact. But one in five of the former, compared with one in fourteen of the latter, were relatively isolated from workmates, with very little or no contact. Thirty-seven per cent of the handicapped, 41 per cent of the special help group, 45 per cent of the would benefit and 61 per cent of the non-handicapped had a lot of contact with their workmates.[15]

The importance of social contact for young people is illustrated by the very significant relationship between extent of social contact and statements about how their experience of work compared with other young people. Those with least social contact were more likely to say that their experience was worse than average (see Chapter 7).[16]

Job security

There has been much written and said about the fact that young people are more prone than older workers to change jobs more frequently. But there is another side to this particular labour market coin: job tenure. This is known to differ broadly according to social class. There are, of course, exceptions, but there are also familiar stereotypes at each end of the scale, the judge and university lecturer enjoying almost total permanence and the casual labourer on, at best, a week's notice. Does the world of work offer young people much security?

Respondents who had worked were asked whether they felt their job was secure or otherwise. The majority (63 per cent) thought that their job was secure. When asked for reasons a large proportion did not give one. There were statistically very significant differences between the handicapped and other groups, and the non-handicapped in their answers to this question, with 68 per cent of the handicapped, 66 per cent of the special help group, 81 per cent of the would benefit group and 84 per cent of the non-handicapped feeling secure. Conversely 32 per cent of the former compared with 15 per cent of the latter felt insecure.[17] Those who were currently unemployed were excluded from these statistics. Not surprisingly their presence had the effect of increasing the sense of insecurity expressed by the sample.

Of the handicapped who felt that their jobs were secure, 16 per cent did so because the firm or business they were working for was doing well (compared with 24 per cent of non-handicapped); 16 per cent because they thought they did their job well (compared with 12 per cent of non-handicapped) and 12 per cent because of the negative reason that there had been no recent redundancies at their place of work (as compared with 12 per cent of non-handicapped). Turning to those handicapped young people who felt insecure, 14 per cent did so because of a lack of work at their employment and 13 per cent because they were doing a temporary job; 20 per cent felt insecure because of the impending threat of redundancy (9 per cent of all handicapped young people in the sample who were in work). In addition, 3 per cent felt insecure because of their handicap.[18]

Why were the handicapped so much more likely than the non-handicapped to feel insecure? Primarily insecurity is a function of the kinds of work and the level of work the handicapped are doing. Young people (and others) are more likely to be made redundant from manual jobs. The experience of unemployment itself is likely to heighten feelings of insecurity in current work. As we have seen, the prevalence of unemployment is highest amongst the handicapped.

There were interesting sexual differences in job security. Nearly, 66 per cent of handicapped males compared with 75 per cent of females felt secure in their job (again those currently unemployed were excluded), but among non-handicapped young people 91 per cent of males and 77 per cent of females felt secure. The main reasons for insecurity given by both groups were lack of work at their shop or factory, temporary work and impending redundancy.[19]

Perceptions of work

A thorough assessment of job satisfaction would involve a separate study, but we wanted a picture of how happy the young people were in work, principally because this must play a crucial role in forming wider attitudes and reactions to work. Dissatisfaction is one obvious reaction to the objective conditions that young people encounter at work. If work is dull, boring, monotonous; if it does not come up to expectation; if it is unrewarding financially and psychologically; if young people are isolated or working in poor conditions, they will probably not be very happy.

Degree of satisfaction with work

One expression of dissatisfaction is the amount of boredom young people say they experience in work. If they are bored or feel they are, their abilities are not being used to the full and their involvement with work is restricted. Expressions of boredom are a well known feature of the literature on young workers. According to the ILO: 'most young industrial workers do not appear to relish their work as an older generation did, and take no interest in it at all. They do it more or less well, as a chore impossible to avoid, and they are inveterate clock-watchers. Time and again this feeling of boredom and dissatisfaction transpires from enquiries. For young people, work is not a way of life but just a job.'[20]

In her study of 15- to 18-year-olds in work, Maizels found 10 per cent of boys and girls reported work to be boring and 19 per cent found it monotonous. Not surprisingly the experience of boredom and monotony was related to job-type, with 16 per cent of manual workers finding their job boring.[21] This problem is therefore more likely to affect the handicapped and disadvantaged and others who occupy the lowest status positions, those in *careerless* jobs. For them 'the main problems are not those of mastering new skills but rather those of learning to cope with their relationships with older workers, their subordinate position at work, and the boredom and monotony of the job.'[22]

Eighteen-year-olds in the sample were asked whether they ever found work boring. Forty-five per cent of the handicapped, 42 per cent of the special help group, 58 per cent of the would benefit group and 34 per cent of the non-handicapped said they were never bored at work.[23] The tendency was for the non-handicapped to be more frequently bored with work, with over half being bored sometimes compared with just over a third of the handicapped. This confirms Carter's finding that duller children are often content to find a niche where they can do all that is asked of them.[24] However, there was a slight tendency for the handicapped to be bored for much of the time – 19 per cent were bored at work *often* or *always*, compared with 11 per cent of the non-handicapped.

In order to assess the degree of satisfaction that the sample were experiencing in their current (or latest) job they were asked, simply, whether or not they were happy in their job. Excluding those currently unemployed, the handicapped were more than twice as likely as the non-handicapped to be *un*happy in their job. Fifteen per cent compared with 6 per cent were not very happy or were very unhappy in their jobs. Differences between the handicapped and non-handicapped were statistically very significant.[25] Physically handicapped young people were the most unhappy of the handicapped, one-third were not very happy or very unhappy. Twenty-five per cent of the maladjusted and 23 per cent of the ESN(M) were also relatively unhappy.

Degree of happiness *was* related to the type of job the young people were doing, though some cell numbers in this analysis were very small. None were very *unhappy* in farming, professional nor clerical work, and only one in engineering and building. Unhappiness was concentrated amongst those in the service and manual industrial sectors. The majority of the handicapped were in these occupations. One-quarter of those (10 out of 38) who were in service occupations were relatively unhappy. Twenty-five per cent of the handicapped in industrial manual jobs were not contented. Of the handicapped young people who were unhappy, all but four were in these occupations. None of the control group were very unhappy, the majority being happy or very happy. Forty-five per cent of this group were in the clerical or engineering sectors.[26]

There was a very significant relationship between job satisfaction and working conditions as indicated by the work facilities index. Those in jobs with six or more facilities were more likely to be happy in their work than those in jobs with fewer facilities. Taking the two main groups only, and the handicapped first, 16 per cent of those who were very happy or were very unhappy had five or fewer of the facilities on the list, while 43 per cent of those who were *not* very happy or were very unhappy had five or fewer of these facilities. Of the handicapped whose employers provided eight or more of the facilities only 7 per cent were relatively unhappy (11 per cent of those with six or more facilities). Among the non-handicapped, only 4 per cent of those with eight or more facilities were not very happy.[27]

The obvious reaction to these worrying statistics on job satisfaction must be attempts to improve the quality of the working environment – especially in the predominantly unskilled and semi skilled jobs that handicapped young people do, a policy that is developed at length in Chapter 14.

Significant job characteristics

The final stage of this analysis of young people in their working environment was an assessment of answers to questions about those aspects of jobs that were considered important or unimportant in *creating* happiness in work. As we have already looked at some reactions or 'attitudes' to work – the degree of happiness and boredom – the answers to these questions give some further indication of the orientation towards work among the 18-year-olds in the sample.

I wanted some idea of the kind of qualities that young people would, ideally, want from work in order to be happy. In the course of their research on school-leavers Thomas and Wetherell had constructed an index to do precisely this.[28] Some changes, into less sophisticated wording, were necessary – for example, 'promotion' became 'getting on' – to cater for the less able young people in the sample. Figure 5.1 shows the division between the predominant concern of the handicapped for the quality of social contact at work and of the non-handicapped for training, followed closely by social factors and pride in work.

The third NCDS follow-up at 16 years of age used a similar list of job characteristics to that of Thomas and Wetherell. Interestingly, over three-quarters of the NCDS sample considered that good pay was an important characteristic, three-fifths counted it among the three most important and one-fifth considered it the most important of all.[29] This can be compared with the non-handicapped group in this sample, which provided a very rough approximation of the whole NCDS group. Just over one twentieth of the non-handicapped mentioned this as being most important. One-fifth of the NCDS sample at 16 thought that 'variety' was most important in a job, compared with one-tenth of the non-handicapped in this study. Amongst the lowest placed at both 16 and 18 was 'the risk of getting dirty'.

There were considerable differences between the handicapped and non-handicapped groups within the NCDS at age 16. For example, 21 per cent of the handicapped compared with 4 per cent of the non-handicapped thought that the most important aspect to be looked for in choosing a job was that work should involve working with one's hands, while 31 per cent of the former and 18 per cent of the latter thought that good pay was the most important. These figures are based on the total numbers in those groups at the time of the follow-up at 16 years of age. Four times the proportion of non-handicapped than handicapped were looking for variety as the most important future job aspect, and twice the proportion thought that the chance to help others was paramount.

Attitudes to work

What do answers to questions about important job characteristics reveal about the young people's attitudes towards work? There are many problems associated with questions of attitude, not least that attitudes may be formed during the course of an interview. Since the majority of the young people were in employment, an answer to these questions would be coloured by their experience at work and particularly their current employment situation. The majority of

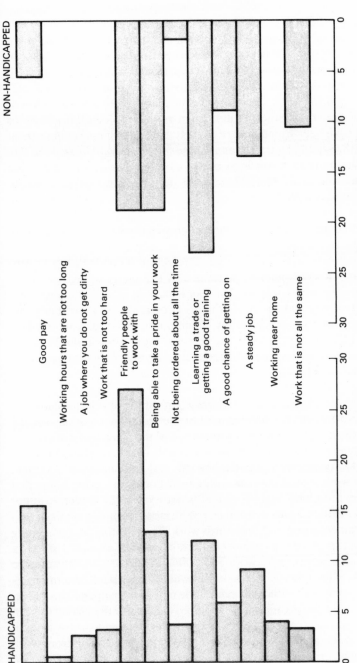

NON-HANDICAPPED

HANDICAPPED

Good pay

Working hours that are not too long

A job where you do not get dirty

Work that is not too hard

Friendly people to work with

Being able to take a pride in your work

Not being ordered about all the time

Learning a trade or getting a good training

A good chance of getting on

A steady job

Working near home

Work that is not all the same

FIGURE 5.1 *Percentage of handicapped and non-handicapped young people nominating different characteristics they would most want in order to be happy in a job*

young people were contacted after decisions relating to their entry into the labour market had been made. This means that we could not investigate the psychological process underlying their choice of occupation. The usefulness of retrospective attitude data has been questioned.[30] However, answers to such questions collected after commencing work are more useful than those collected prior to entry into the labour market, when any psychological orientations will have been framed out of context, and when young people are at the threshold of a transitional phase of their development.

Orientations towards work are closely related to the type and status of employment. There are wide variations, but according to Thomas and Wetherell:

> A contrast frequently appears between two extreme groups, with the remainder of the population ranged along a continuum between them. At the one extreme are individuals whose attitude towards jobs is determined by the nature of the work itself – its intrinsic interest, the scope for individuals skill, authority, creativity and so on. At the other extreme are individuals who appear to start from the assumption that the work itself is unlikely to offer them any personal satisfaction and that consequently the less physical and mental involvement they have in it, the better.[31]

These groups are typified in Lockwood's study of working class attitudes to work: the involvement of the traditional worker and the 'extrinsic' or instrumental orientation of the *privatised* worker.[32]

Some of the items on the list of job characteristics indicate a preoccupation with material rewards and a minimum involvement with work: 'good pay', 'working near home', 'working hours that are not too long' and 'work that is not too hard'.[33] Taken together they might indicate – it can be put no more strongly than that – an *instrumental orientation* towards work. Those young people naming these aspects of jobs as most important could be expected to have a low involvement with work and to find their main interests outside work. Altogether 23 per cent of the handicapped fell into this category compared with 5 per cent of the non-handicapped. This difference reflected the tendency, reported earlier, for the former to be in jobs of a lower social class than the latter. Young workers with an instrumental orientation are most likely to be alienated from work (indeed this attitude could be defined as alienation.[34] They are likely to be less interested in training, further education and a traditional career, and perhaps be less inclined to put much effort into choosing a job. They correspond broadly to those young people with a 'careerless' perspective described by Ashton and Field.[35]

There is evidence of a decline in instrumentality once the world of work has been encountered. At the age of 16 33 per cent of the handicapped took an instrumental view, and 23 per cent of the non-handicapped (compared with 23 per cent and 5 per cent respectively at 18). But the questions used for the surveys of 16- and 18-year-olds were not exactly the same, and in the former, 'attitudes' were formed before entry into the labour market.[36]

Other items on the list of job characteristics could be taken to indicate – again this is not suggesting a refined and tested scale or index – an opposing view of work. Those placing most importance on being able to take a pride in their work, learning a trade or getting good training and a good chance of getting on came close to a *work* or *career orientation*. Young people holding this view are likely to be more personally involved with work than the instrumental, privatised worker. It suggests that work for them may have more intrinsic rewards and be a potential source of satisfaction. These young workers are prepared to give more physical and mental involvement to work. Nearly 31 per cent of handicapped 18-year-olds and 50 per cent of the non-handicapped were in this group.[37]

Interrelationship between objective and subjective aspects of the work situation

As expected, social class exerted a strong influence on attitudes to work. Amongst the handicapped actually in employment, for example, four out of five of those with an instrumental orientation towards work were in the two lowest classes (semi-skilled and unskilled manual). On the other hand, one-third of those with a career orientation were in the skilled manual and non-manual groups. The proportion in each social class with an instrumental orientation towards work increased gradually as the level of the class fell.

Some of the detailed differences are easier to assimilate if social class is divided into manual and non-manual groups only. Looking at the handicapped first, more of the non-manual than manual wanted to learn a trade and to get on (twice the proportion of the manual group) and more looked for friendly people (29 per cent compared with 16 per cent). The proportion of manual workers saying that pay was the most important aspect of a job was four times that for the non-manual sector. Turning to non-handicapped young people, none of the non-manual workers said that pay was most important, while 4 per cent of manual workers did. Twenty-nine per cent compared with 18 per cent looked for friendly people. However, 16 per cent of the manual workers and 6 per cent of the non-manual workers said that being able to take a pride in their work was most important and 39 per cent and 10 per cent respectively said that learning a trade was most important.[38] These latter differences reflect the importance of apprenticeships among non-handicapped manual workers.

Having established a relationship between orientation towards work and social class it seemed probable that the former would also be related to satisfaction with work. Despite the small numbers among the non-handicapped, analysis showed that the two variables were related. Not surprisingly perhaps, those who are relatively unhappy at work are most likely to value extrinsic factors in their working life. On the other hand, those who are very happy are more likely to value intrinsic factors. Seventeen per cent of the handicapped young people who were very happy in their job took an instrumental view of work and 34 per cent a career orientation. But for those who were unhappy in their job the figures were 39 per cent and 19 per cent. None of the non-handicapped who were very happy took an instrumental view, yet 60 per cent had a career orientation towards work. Forty per cent of the non-handicapped who were unhappy in their job thought that extrinsic factors were most important.[39]

Finally, the interrelationship between orientation towards work and working conditions provides further evidence that attitudes are partly shaped by and in turn contribute to the young persons' experience of work. Nearly two-fifths of the handicapped with an instrumental orientation towards work, were in jobs where employers provided five or fewer of the facilities on our list. An equal proportion of the handicapped who valued intrinsic factors were in jobs providing eight or more facilities. So those handicapped young people working in relatively poor conditions were more likely to take an instrumental view of work than those in jobs with good facilities. The proportion of handicapped young people in jobs with few facilities who held an instrumental attitude towards work was twice that of those in jobs with relatively good working conditions.[40]

It was encouraging to find that while relatively small proportions of the sample of handicapped and non-handicapped young people took an instrumental view, significantly large groups did not. Equal proportions of both groups agreed that pay, hours and dirty work were least important. Whether this was an unreal or temporary attitude is open to speculation. What was disturbing, however, was the difference between the handicapped and non-handicapped in attitudes, just as the underlying differences in job status and conditions were disturbing. If such inequalities are maintained many of the handicapped young people are destined to become the older disillusioned, alienated workers of the future.

Summary

This description of the working conditions, facilities and attitudes to work of the 18-year-olds has shown that the handicapped were poorly placed in relation to the non-handicapped. They were less likely to travel for long periods to work, but more likely to work long hours – three-quarters of them were working over 40 hours compared with nearly two-thirds of the control group. The handicapped were twice as likely as the non-handicapped to be doing heavy lifting all or nearly all of their time. Two-and-a-half times the proportion of handicapped young people compared with non-handicapped had few work-based facilities; they were four times as unlikely to have most facilities. Those with fewer facilities were more likely than those with better facilities to be unhappy in work. The handicapped were often isolated from their workmates at this critical period of post-school development. They were more likely than the non-handicapped to feel insecure and much more likely to be relatively unhappy. Some of these statistics are disturbing to the extent that they reveal a considerable inequality between the handicapped and non-handicapped young people in their experience of day to day working life.

6

Job Aspirations before and after Labour Market Entry

One important aspect of labour market experiences is whether young people achieve or fail to achieve any expectations they formed prior to starting work, and whether they have ambitions beyond their present employment. Failure to realise their aspirations may be one reason why young people were already dissatisfied with work after only two years in the labour market. In addition it was suggested by some careers advisers that handicapped young people often had unrealistic ambitions and that this was a major contributory factor to their relative lack of success in employment. Did the handicapped young people in our sample have unrealistic ambitions? This chapter looks at the aspirations of handicapped young people in conjunction with their non-handicapped peers, goes on to assess them in relation to ability and finally attempts to answer some of the questions begged by the analysis.

It is clearly pre-emptive to expect ambitions to be realised after only two years in the labour market. It is therefore necessary to distinguish between aspirations and preferences. The latter represent a job or job area that is desired, if other conditions allow, while the former is taken to mean a longer term ambition or target. Job preferences must in turn be distinguished from predictions based on an assessment of the most likely outcome.

At the third follow-up, the NCDS collected both types of information: from young people, their desired and likely future occupation; from teachers, the young persons' expected area of work, and from parents the desired and likely areas of work. Analysis of parents' answers is reserved for Chapter 13. In addition to the information from the NCDS details were also collected of ideal or 'wish' jobs, to determine the existence of any unrealistic ambitions.

Teachers' predictions

At the third NCDS follow-up, teachers were asked what they thought were likely to be the young peoples' first jobs (but not the status or skill level). Results show that parents', young persons' and teachers' prediction of likely job areas were very similar.[1] Out of those actually in work at the time of interview (that is, excluding those in further education and those who were not working) 31 per cent of the handicapped and 29 per cent of the non-handicapped were in the type of job predicted by the teachers; 32 per cent and 23 per cent respectively were working in broadly the predicted area of work and 37 per cent and 47 per cent respectively were in completely different jobs.[2] These statistics refer to current or last jobs, and thus allow for any settling down period. Secondly, the classifications of job area are very broad, including 'service' and 'manual (industrial)' so increasing the chances of successful prediction.

Job preferences and expectations

Turning now to the young person's aims: at 16 they were asked what type of job they would *like* to have and then what type of job they thought they were *likely* to do. Table 6.1 shows the job areas that young people desired, expected and then got on entry into the labour market.

Table 6.1 illustrates a number of important facts. First, the non-handicapped as a group aspired to, expected and eventually obtained a greater proportion of professional, managerial and clerical, (that is, white-collar) jobs. Differences between the handicapped and non-handicapped in the type of jobs *desired* and expected were statistically very significant. The handicapped were less likely to expect professional jobs and more likely to expect manual industrial jobs. Differences between the handicapped and non-handicapped in the type of *first* job held were also very significant.

On the evidence of first jobs, the jobs desired by the handicapped were no more unrealistic than those desired by the non-handicapped and perhaps a good deal less so.[3] A recent study of school-leavers in Scotland found that disadvantaged boys lowered their sights from 'dream' jobs to 'hope' jobs more drastically than others. 'This finding was irrespective of ability or school progress and shows how feelings of deprivation can affect aspirations'.[4] The tendency

TABLE 6.1 *Comparison of desired, expected and first jobs (%)*

Occupational group of desired expected first job	Sample group			
	Handi-capped	Special help	Would benefit	Non-handi-capped
	7.4	7.8	3.4	4.7
Farming and outdoor	6.3	10.1	5.3	4.6
	7.6	10.9	0.0	3.7
Professional and	12.3	14.7	17.2	36.7
managerial	5.1	9.0	9.4	25.5
	0.0	3.1	2.0	12.5
	19.0	20.6	12.6	9.4
Service	18.6	21.3	14.7	10.8
	22.8	25.0	23.5	21.2
	7.8	4.9	6.9	13.3
Clerical	6.7	3.4	5.3	17.0
	4.3	6.2	5.9	22.5
	42.2	42.1	46.0	25.7
Manual (Industrial)	41.7	37.0	49.3	23.2
	52.8	54.7	64.6	33.7
	11.1	9.8	12.6	10.2
Other	21.5	19.1	16.0	18.6
	12.5	0.0	3.9	6.2
Total	100	100	100	100
	242	102	87	128
Number	237	89	75	129
	184	64	51	80

Handicapped *vs* non-handicapped:
desired job: $X^2 = 38.89$, 5 degrees of freedom, $p < 0.001$
expected job: $X^2 = 48.69$, 5 degrees of freedom, $p < 0.001$
first job: $X^2 = 43.98$, 5 degrees of freedom, $p < 0.001$

for the general level of aspirations to be higher than achievements was also reported by Maizels. She found 'a reduction in the average level of skill, training, further education and status provided by the jobs actually entered, compared with what would have been offered by those originally preferred'.[5] Incidentally the gap between aims and fulfilment widened further on the basis of subsequent job changes – with a general shift *downwards* in skill level and status.

Differences between the subgroups of handicapped young people, in the jobs they desired at the age of 16, emphasised the relationship between disadvantage and educational (rather than physical) handicap and preferences for low status jobs. Fifty per cent of the maladjusted wanted jobs in the industrial manual sector. Of the ESN(M) 41 per cent desired such jobs, 22 per cent wanted service jobs and 8 per cent professional jobs. But only 28 per cent of the physically handicapped wanted industrial manual jobs, 20 per cent clerical jobs and 16 per cent service jobs.[6]

Sex differences

The non-handicapped illustrated the clear sexual differences in occupational preference and achievement. Forty-five per cent of the young women desired professional or managerial jobs at the age of 16 compared with 17 per cent of men; 21 per cent of women wanted clerical jobs and 43 per cent of men wanted industrial manual jobs.[8] There were also considerable sexual differences in achievements subsequent to entry into the labour market. Among the handicapped, roughly equal proportions of males and females were in the same type of job at the age of 18 as they desired when they were 16. But males were three times as likely as females to be in jobs in the same group as they had wanted (33 per cent of males and 37 per cent of females were in quite different jobs). Non-handicapped females were twice as likely to be in different jobs as males.[9] There is a clear indication here that whether handicapped or non-handicapped, women are less likely than men to fulfil the broad preferences they hold prior to entering the labour market.

Handicapped preferences

Previous research findings support the conclusion that the differences between the handicapped and non-handicapped shown in Table 6.1 are based on occupational class differences. For example, Maizels found that there was considerable variation between occupational groups in the achievement of aspirations. A much higher proportion of apprentices among boys, and of office workers among girls, were in jobs more or less identical to their first preferences (over half) than was the case among leavers in relatively unskilled manual work.[10] Over half of these boys and three-quarters of girls were in jobs that differed from their original preference.

Various studies suggest that aspirations are quite unhelpful when expressed out of context, with little knowledge of labour market opportunities.[11] What is surprising, therefore, is the significant proportion who did succeed in achieving their aspiration. An important factor here, particularly among the handicapped is the general low level of job preferences. It may be that handicapped young people are better than we think at assimilating a large amount of knowledge about their own abilities and the structure of opportunities and forming them into job preferences and expectations. Furthermore, it would appear that young people adjust their preferences towards jobs which they think they can obtain and that are appropriate for them.[12] Clearly schools are important in socialising young people in the opportunity structure. The reality of this structure and the differential distribution of young people in it is explored fully in the next three chapters. So far we have been concerned with predictions, desires and expectations concerning employment when the young people were 16. What of their aspirations at 18, formed after they had entered the labour market?

Ideal jobs and ambitions

Carter distinguished between 'fantasy' jobs and 'ideal' jobs. School-leavers were asked: 'If you could do just what job you would like, what would you choose?' 'Fantasy' jobs were those associated with day-dreaming and were part of another world – 'if only' – while 'ideal' jobs were those preferred to the ones proposed. 'The distinction between fantasy and ideal jobs rests upon the child's circumstances rather than the nature of the job.'[13] Some of the reasons given for not aiming at ideal jobs were: lack of ability, bad health, lack of qualifications and few vacancies. Weir and Nolan distinguished 'dream' jobs (based on a free choice), 'hope' jobs (those that the young people would like and think they would not get) and 'real' jobs (those that they think they will have to take). Almost half their sample dreamed and hoped for 'professional' or 'entertainment' types of employment. 'When it came down to reality, however, reason prevailed. The boys knew that good jobs would be hard to find, and most choices were spread among the higher-status skilled employment.'[14] The authors note that the boys' personal experience at the time of the interview was limited and this is borne out by the current research which indicated that aspirations were rather ambitious.

In order to explore the extent of any differences in ambitions all respondents were asked what would they *most* like to do if they were free to choose *any* job. To encourage a note of realism and avoid fantasy choices we added that it should be a job with which they felt they could cope. Answers to this question were coded according to class as well as job type. Table 6.2 indicates the wide differences in the level of aspirations between the handicapped and non-handicapped. These differences were statistically very significant. While the majority of the handicapped aspired to jobs of skilled manual level or below, the majority of non-handicapped aspired to jobs of skilled level or above.

TABLE 6.2 *Social class of ideal jobs (%)*

Level of job	Sample group			
	Handi-capped	Special help	Would benefit	Non-handi-capped
Professional, managerial	1.5	4.3	1.8	8.8
Intermediate	8.7	7.2	13.0	24.8
Skilled non-manual	7.1	11.6	9.2	4.4
Skilled manual	26.5	27.5	31.5	15.9
Semi-skilled non-manual	5.6	4.3	5.5	4.4
Semi-skilled manual	12.2	2.9	1.8	3.5
Unskilled	4.6	2.9	0.0	0.0
Forces	3.1	2.9	5.5	1.8
Other[a]	20.9	11.6	16.7	12.4
Current job[b]	9.7	24.6	14.8	23.9
Total	100	100	100	100
Number	196	69	54	113

Handicapped *vs* non-handicapped:
$X^2 = 39.09$, 5 degrees of freedom, $p < 0.001$.
[a] Includes 'don't know', 'no information', unclassifiable.
[b] Those whose ideal job was the job they were currently doing are classified under 'current job'. Others were classified according to the social class of the ideal job, even when this was the same social class as their current job.

Among the handicapped sub-groups only 3 out of 27 physically handicapped said they would have liked intermediate or professional jobs. The same applies to 7 per cent of the ESN(M) but 25 per cent (8 out of 31) of the maladjusted.[15] Ironically the latter came closest to the aspirations of the non-handicapped. This is a significant finding when taken in conjunction with the greater propensity for this group to be underemployed (see Chapter 7).

Rather than finding unrealistically high ambitions it was the low level of aspirations of the majority of the handicapped compared to the non-handicapped that was remarkable and contrary to expectations. Of course a proper assessment of the realism of those aspirations depends on a detailed analysis of abilities and a start is made on this later in the Chapter. Carter also found that the aspirations of children of low ability and low attainment were essentially realistic (in contrast to the findings of Weir and Nolan in Scotland). Both Carter and Veness remarked on the low level of ambition among secondary modern school-leavers. Fewer than 10 per cent of the 200 Sheffield boys and girls whom Carter studied had serious job ambitions which they had no hope of fulfilling. The aspirations of many were 'incredibly' low – many were 'not bothered' about the type of work.[16]

The next stage of this analysis was to compare the ideal job aspirations of the young people with their present employment. Incongruity between the two might have laid the foundation for dissatisfaction arising from unfulfilled ambition. Surprisingly, the same proportion of handicapped and non-handicapped young people (42 per cent) did not aspire to types of jobs different from their present job. Similar proportions aspired to different types of jobs (38 per cent and 33 per cent). The figures for the two less handicapped groups from ordinary schools were also roughly similar – 52 per cent of the special help group and 55 per cent of the would benefit group wanted jobs in the same occupational group while 42 per cent and 41 per cent wanted different jobs.[17]

Of course this congruence between handicapped and non-handicapped young people does not mean that the two groups aspired to jobs at exactly the same category or level, for when we turned to the social class of ideal jobs compared to actual jobs, a much higher degree of incongruity was revealed (see Table 6.3). While 35 per cent of handicapped young people had ideal jobs in the same social class as their current jobs, 56 per cent of the non-handicapped were in this position. Conversely, 64 per cent of the former and 44 per cent

TABLE 6.3 *Social class of ideal job compared with actual job (%)*

Social class of latest job[a]	Handicapped			Non-handicapped		
	Ideal compared with actual job class					
	Same	Different	Total	Same	Different	Total
Professional and intermediate	(0.0)	0.0	0.0	(18.6)	(2.9)	11.7
Skilled non-manual	(12.2)	9.0	10.2	(16.3)	(52.9)	32.5
Skilled manual	(30.6)	12.4	19.3	(48.8)	(17.6)	35.1
Semi-skilled	(46.9)	46.1	46.6	(13.9)	(20.6)	16.9
Unskilled	(10.2)	32.6	23.9	(2.3)	(5.9)	3.9
Total	100	100	100	100	100	100
Number	49	89	138	43	34	77

For handicapped group: $X^2 = 12.35$, 3 degrees of freedom, $p < 0.01$
For non-handicapped group: $X^2 = 8.11$, 3 degrees of freedom, $p < 0.05$
Grouping of social class: professional, intermediate, skilled; non-manual; skilled manual; semi-skilled; unskilled.
[a] Current or latest job, excludes those who had not worked or who were unemployed.

of the latter wanted jobs in a different (not necessarily higher) social class. Differences between the handicapped and non-handicapped were statistically very significant.[18] Males were more likely than females to aspire to jobs of a different status.[19]

Handicapped aspirations

Comparisons between the handicapped and non-handicapped are illuminating in tracing the relative disadvantage of handicapped young people. In both groups the skilled manual workers were more likely than not to aspire to jobs in the same social class. They were the most content. The lowest skilled were the most discontented and therefore the handicapped much more so, because a greater proportion of them were semi-skilled and unskilled than the non-handicapped. Handicapped young people whose current jobs were of skilled level, were more likely not to aspire beyond their current job than those in semi-skilled and unskilled work (29 per cent, compared with 17 per cent). If they did aspire to other jobs these were of a slightly higher level than those to which the less skilled aspired. Fourteen per cent compared with 9 per cent aspired to the professional and intermediate classes, while 18 per cent and 23 per cent aspired to jobs in the semi-skilled and unskilled classes (these figures exclude those not working). So, 67 per cent of the unskilled, 66 per cent of the semi-skilled and 60 per cent of the skilled manual handicapped young people did not aspire to jobs in social classes above the skilled manual level.

The experience of unemployment, perhaps not surprisingly, had the effect of further reducing aspirations. Thus, in addition to the relatively low aspirations of handicapped young workers, handicapped young people who were currently unemployed were twice as likely as those working, to aspire to jobs in the lowest two social classes, and four times as likely as the non-handicapped to do so.[20]

Carter has argued that because school-leavers' aspirations were low: 'This means that for the majority of leavers the transition to work does not involve disappointment or dissatisfaction with the type of job obtained'.[23] But the data outlined above indicate that a substantial proportion of the handicapped and a smaller proportion of the non-handicapped, feel that they could cope with the ideal jobs of a different type and status to the ones in which they were currently employed, and suggest a very different picture of early labour market experiences to that presented by Carter. In turn this reinforces the differences in satisfaction with work shown in Chapter 5.

Aspirations and ability

Were the ambitions of the handicapped and others of 'low ability' unrealistic? In other words did they aspire to jobs that were beyond their abilities? These questions were tackled in the certain knowledge that complete answers, on the basis of the information at our disposal, were impossible. To obtain them would need detailed information not only about the abilities of the young people but also about the skills required to do the jobs to which they aspired. But this survey was better placed than many studies of school-leavers in being able to draw objective conclusions about abilities. First, there were estimates of ability in the most important school subjects. At the third NCDS follow-up, teachers were asked to note the child's ability in certain subjects, including maths and English. Secondly, in this survey three measures of functional ability were used. The young people were rated according to their ability in self-care, social communication, and participation and employment functions.

Teachers' ratings of ability were split into 'average and above' and 'below average'. Obviously (since handicap is defined in educational terms) the vast majority of the handicapped were rated by teachers as being below average. When those in further education were excluded there was no difference in the proportion of handicapped of above- and below-average ability who aspired to a different social class.[22] However, when the level of aspirations was examined, ability emerged as a more important determining factor. Only 17 per cent of handicapped young people aspired to jobs in social classes above the level of skilled manual. But 45 per cent of the handicapped of average or above-average ability in maths, aspired to the higher social classes – compared with 13 per cent of those of below-average ability. Handicapped young people of below-average ability formed a decreasing proportion of the handicapped of all levels of ability who aspired to higher and higher social classes. The majority of those whose ideal job was their current job were of below-average ability in maths.[23]

A similar picture was revealed by looking at teachers' ratings in English, where the majority of the handicapped were also rated as being of below-average ability. Similar proportions of handicapped young people who aspired to jobs in the same or different social classes, were above and below-average ability in English. The major tendency was for those who were above the average ability to aspire to a higher social class. Here, importantly, very few of those handicapped young people of below-average ability, aspired to jobs above the skilled manual level. Statistically significant differences *within* the handicapped group were obtained by combining professional, intermediate and skilled classes (because of small numbers).[25]

Reference to functional abilities further illustrated the fact that the least-able are less likely to aspire to the non-manual classes. Thus, the handicapped who scored on the social communication scale were less likely to aspire to the highest social classes and much more likely to aspire to the lowest. Differences were statistically significant.[26] Three-quarters of those whose ideal jobs were in the semi-skilled and unskilled manual classes had some handicap on the social communication and participation index. So, on the basis of the information available, there were strong indications that the very few handicapped young people who did aspire to the higher, non-manual social classes, were more likely to be of higher ability than the rest of their peer group.

Social determinants of low aspirations

In Chapter 5 the handicapped were shown to be more unhappy and dissatisfied with work than were the non-handicapped. This was clearly an important reason why they aspired to jobs of a different class; their failure to realise such aspirations in turn reinforced their dissatisfaction. But why were their aspirations so low?

Perhaps, primarily, low aspirations represent an adaptation to reality as perceived by the young person. Thus handicapped young people internalise the judgements of the school, home and the rest of society about their abilities and potential. They are destined to enter, if they are lucky, semi-skilled and unskilled employment. This, then, is for them the reality of work. They may be 'careerless'[27] but this is merely a reflection and internalisation of the social construction of the work setting and opportunity structure. They go on from school to occupy a low status in the labour market and are convinced that they will not get jobs above a certain level. This is reflected in their aspirations. A spell of unemployment simply reinforces their low status and low aspirations.

Such low ambitions indicate a prior process of self-evaluation and selection – the setting of a ceiling. The young person's family background is crucial here since it provides his main insight into the world of work. As Thomas and Wetherell have pointed out:

> The applicants for a given job-vacancy will never constitute a cross-section of the full range of academic ability, even if they are school-leavers with no direct experience of the world of employment. It is not so much that barely-literate 15-year-old leavers apply for trainee managerial or professional jobs and are rejected, as that they seldom apply in the first place. This may, indeed, be because they assume that they would be rejected if they did apply. However, there is reason to suppose that many individuals do not set their level of occupational aspiration in any very rational or conscious way, having regard to the range of opportunities actually available. *It is rather that the history and development of their vocational thinking is such that it simply never occurs to them to aspire to a job above – or below – some given level.*[28]

In theory one of the major tasks and problems of vocational guidance is to overcome many such ingrained assumptions about the range of possible occupations, but this assumes that there are alternative avenues of employment for the handicapped and others of limited educational achievement to follow.

Thomas and Wetherell found that academic ability, diligence and success at school were associated with a generally high level of aspiration (prior to labour market entry). Thus, 'those who know or feel themselves to be (academically) successful will (justifiably) tend to aspire higher in vocational terms, while the opposite applies to those who are academically unsuccessful'.[29]

Those who are at or are near the lower end of the ability continuum form their aspirations on the basis of their perception of their own abilities. Such perceptions rely on judgements from home, peer group and particularly the schools. To quote the authors of the Office of Population Censuses and Surveys study again: 'There is (thus) a possibility that teachers' opinions of boys' academic potential actually function to some extent as causal factors in determining each boy's level of vocational, as well as academic, aspiration.'[30] This is of fundamental importance. If schools, especially special schools, limit – intentionally or otherwise – the extent of the handicapped young person's aspirations, it is not surprising that there is a difference between the handicapped and non-handicapped.

Handicapped young people, more often than the non-handicapped, obtained jobs of the type their teachers had predicted before they left school. It may be that there is a process akin to a self-fulfilling prophecy in operation here, linking predictions with aspirations and outcome. No firm conclusions can be offered on this score. What is clear, however, is that the aspirations of the handicapped were depressed in relation to those of the non-handicapped and when they were above average, this was supported by above-average ability.

Summary

The non-handicapped preferred, expected and eventually got a greater proportion of white-collar jobs than did the handicapped. One-fifth of the handicapped compared with one-third of the non-handicapped had by the age of 18 achieved the jobs they had desired at 16. Over one-third of handicapped young people and one-quarter of non-handicapped were in different jobs from those they had desired.

The aspirations of handicapped young people were incredibly low. The proportion of non-handicapped aspiring to professional, managerial or intermediate jobs was three times that of the handicapped. At the same time the proportion of the latter aspiring to semi-skilled and unskilled jobs was six times that of the former. In addition there was enormous incongruity among the handicapped, and to a lesser extent the non-handicapped, between 'aspired' job status and current job status. Nearly two thirds of those non-handicapped who had worked since leaving school wanted jobs in a different social class, compared with 44 per cent of the handicapped. But the highest aspiration of the majority of the handicapped young people in unskilled or semi-skilled jobs was the skilled manual class. Those in skilled manual jobs were more content than the semi-skilled and unskilled. The aspirations of the handicapped could not be labelled unrealistic. They wanted jobs of a different status, but not very different.

7

Occupational Choice and Careers Advice

The transition of young people from school to work is usually considered to be a crucial stage in the individual's development. Research effort has concentrated on careers advice, the Careers Service and entry into employment, rather than on the objective conditions that young people experience once in work. Yet as Roberts has commented: 'No amount of guidance can change the realities of work in an industrial society.'[1]

As part of this investigation of 18-year-olds details were sought of careers teaching received in school and about careers advice interviews with careers officers. In this chapter the results of these questions are considered together with information collected concerning sources of information about job vacancies, agencies used to find jobs, type of first job and reasons for taking particular jobs. The influence of careers advice on job stability and on the proportion of time spent in work is analysed in Chapters 8 and 9.

Occupational choice and class structure

An influential body of theory in the study of vocational choice, stemming from the work of Ginzberg and Super, holds that choice between different jobs is based on individual ambition.[2] Although we did not set out to test the validity of developmental theories of occupational choice,[3] results presented so far do not indicate the presence of any realistic choice in the kinds of jobs done by the 18-year-olds. It is hard to believe that given a free choice such significant percentages of young people would enter semi-skilled and unskilled jobs, rather than more rewarding skilled and non-manual tasks. The data on satisfaction with work analysed in Chapter 5 supports this conclusion.

Respondents who were working or who had worked since leaving school were also asked what were the most important reasons for taking their current or last job. Twenty-six per cent of the sample said that it was the only job available or the first job offered, 18 per cent said that the money was good and 29 per cent said that the type of work appealed to them. Results (analysed according to each handicapped group) in Table 7.1 (p. 80) show that it was the educationally unqualified handicapped young people who were most likely to say that their latest job was the only job available or was the first one offered. These findings appear to support the conclusion that different groups of school-leavers are presented with different opportunity structures. Thus according to Roberts: 'The close relationship between the educational status of school-leavers and the status of their first jobs implies no differences in the vocational attitudes, ideals and values of different groups of school-leavers. Different attainments can be accounted for in terms of differential opportunity structures.'[4] In their investigation of prospective school-leavers, Thomas and Wetherell found that some of those with jobs fixed-up never actually chose the jobs in the sense of preferring them to alternatives: they may have been a last resort or have been fixed up by a relative or friend.[5]

To explain the occupations that people are in we must therefore examine not only the processes whereby individuals may exercise a preferential choice but also the processes whereby some individual and not others are accepted for different jobs.[6] The attitudes of employers in this survey are examined in Chapter 10, but as we have already noted, the process which sorts young people into different levels or occupational classes begins long before face-to-face contact with employers begins. Thus the pool of applicants for any job never reflects the entire population of those who need work, nor of those who couyld do the jobs;[7] it is clearly the culmination of a process of social selection.

It is perhaps most helpful to imagine a continuum of occupational choice which depends primarily on social class and educational achievement (sex, handicap and ethnic origins are other significant dimensions within this overall pattern of class variation). Those at one extreme of the continuum have limited choice, between different jobs of the same low occupational status, while those at the other have a much wider choice. In a period of high unemployment the 'choice' of the former may become no choice at all. The educational system provides a channelling mechanism which in general translates status differences into educational qualifications and thereby sorts children into hierarchical groups. Paradoxically in a welfare state, most teaching effort and resources go to those at the top of this hierarchy, the most able. In any general picture there are of course important variations, for example, the influence that a mother of middle-class origins but in a working-class family may have on her child's educational achievement.

Many of the 18-year-olds in the sample will soon become parents themselves and on the basis of findings reported so far, it would not be surprising if many of them pass on to their children an image of society and work which emphasises the importance of short-term rewards rather than deferred gratification. As subsequent chapters reveal in detail, handicapped young people were more likely than the non-handicapped to experience instability in their first two years of employment and the image of work that they pass on to their children will probably reflect this lack of security.

Transition from school to work

Turning to the analysis of our survey data, non-handicapped young people were more likely than the handicapped to have obtained a job immediately after leaving school, and non-handicapped young men more often than women. Fifty-four per cent of the physically handicapped, 71 per cent of the ESN(M) and 70 per cent of the maladjusted, compared with 87 per cent of men in the control group and 76 per cent of women in this group got jobs immediately on leaving school. Twelve per cent of the physically handicapped, 5 per cent of the ESN(M), 11 per cent of the maladjusted and 2 per cent of the non-handicapped were unemployed for three months or more after leaving school.[8] In their study carried out in the late 1950s Ferguson and Kerr found that only 10 per cent of young people handicapped by cardiac disabilities failed to find work within eight weeks of leaving school.[9]

Young people who had worked since leaving school were asked how they felt about their first few days at work and how long it was before they felt accepted by their new colleagues. Fifty per cent of the handicapped (compared with 40 per cent of the non-handicapped) said that the transition to work had been difficult and 30 per cent said it had been easy. The ESN(M) most often found the transition difficult – 57 per cent compared with 54 per cent of the physically handicapped and 32 per cent of the maladjusted. The latter were more likely to have said that the transition from school to work was easy.[10]

The young people were also asked how they thought that their experience of leaving school and finding work compared with that of the average young person. There were very significant differences between the sample groups in their subjective assessments of the transition from school to work, which reflected their objective experiences. While nine out of ten non-handicapped young people said they had done as well as, or better than, average, this applied to three in five of the handicapped. One in twelve of the former compared with one in six of the latter thought they had fared worse than average.[11]

Among the handicapped, those who found the transition from school to work difficult were more likely to have been working in unskilled jobs (23 per cent) compared with those that found it easy (12 per cent).[12]

Table 6.1 showed that non-handicapped young people were much more likely than the handicapped to go into professional or clerical first jobs and less likely to go into manual industrial (but not engineering jobs) jobs. The differences between the handicapped and non-handicapped were statistically very significant.

Sources of information

How did young people find work? Detailed questions were asked about all the jobs that the young people had held since leaving school. Similarly small proportions of both handicapped and non-handicapped had used the Careers Service, but more of the handicapped used informal channels such as relatives and friends or called on the off-chance at employers. More of the non-handicapped than handicapped used newspaper advertisements.

Agencies were used to find jobs according to the type of work in question, with clear differences emerging between manual and non-manual young workers. Manual jobs were frequently found through parents or other relatives and friends, and non-manual jobs were most frequently found through the Careers Service and newspapers. Sixty-one per cent of handicapped young people in manual jobs had used parents, other relatives and friends to find work compared with 31 per cent of *non*-handicapped young people in manual work (more than one agency could have been counted): 28 per cent and 35 per cent respectively had used the Careers Service and 18 per cent and 21 per cent respectively used newspapers. By contrast, 29 per cent of handicapped young people in non-manual work and 33 per cent of non-handicapped young people in non-manual work used parents, other relatives and friends to find jobs. Fifty-two per cent and 23 per cent had used the Careers Service and 10 per cent and 29 per cent had used newspapers.[13]

In hearing about, and finding, jobs, informal channels were of most importance to the majority of the less skilled handicapped young people. Those in unskilled work were nearly four times as likely as the skilled to have heard about their job by calling on employers without appointment; more than six times as likely to have heard from friends and twice as likely as the skilled to have used a job centre.[14]

Did anyone *help* the young person to get a job? Thirty-eight per cent of the handicapped said that they did not receive any help in getting their current job while 18 per cent were helped by a careers officer, 14 per cent by parents, 9 per cent by other relatives, 8 per cent by friends and 6 per cent by a teacher.[15] There were differences between the social classes in the receipt of help: the non-manual were more likely to be helped by the Careers Service (29 per cent compared with 16 per cent of the manual) and the manual workers by parents and relatives (26 per cent compared with 10 per cent of the non-manual workers). Although equal proportions of both occupational groups of handicapped young people received no help there was a difference within the non-handicapped group, with 55 per cent of the non-manual and 36 per cent of the manual workers having received no help.

Occupational choice

Why did young people take the jobs they were working in, or had last worked in? Table 7.1 shows that the handicapped were more likely than the non-handicapped to take jobs because there was no choice, and less likely to take them for reasons associated with the work itself.

Among the handicapped there were, again, wide variations based on social class. The skilled (manual and non-manual) were three times as likely as the unskilled to have said that security was the most important reason (unskilled jobs are of course, the least secure) and nearly four times as likely to say that the type of work was most important. On the other hand, the unskilled were three times as likely as the skilled to have said that pay was most important and twice as likely to say that it was the only job available or first one offered (48 per cent compared with 24 per cent).[16]

TABLE 7.1 *Reasons for taking latest job (%)*

| Most important reason for taking latest job | Sample group | | | |
	Handi-capped	Special help	Would benefit	Non-handi-capped
Secure job	6.4	9.4	5.9	17.5
Good pay	18.0	21.9	27.4	10.0
Type of work	22.7	26.6	27.4	46.2
Near to home	5.8	4.7	7.8	3.7
Only job available	32.0	29.7	23.5	13.7
Friends/relatives working there[a]	3.5	1.6	5.9	3.7
Other	6.4	3.1	2.0	2.5
No reason/don't know	5.2	3.1	0.0	2.5
Total	100	100	100	100
Number	172	64	51	80

[a] Includes two physically handicapped and one ESN(M) who took the jobs for health reasons.

Careers advice

Many young people received advice from different sources, so a summary variable was constructed to show the most *informed* careers advice that the young person received. It is assumed that careers officers and careers teachers are more expert than parents or friends; in most cases they are, of course, but the latter may have more information about job vacancies in the plant or factory in which they work. Handicapped young people were slightly less likely than non-handicapped young people to have seen a careers officer – 75 per cent compared with 80 per cent.

Similarly-small proportions of both groups had received careers advice from a careers teacher (9 per cent and 7 per cent), from other teachers (7 per cent) and from relatives or friends (8 per cent and 6 per cent) as their most informed sources of advice. Differences between the two main sample groups were not significant statistically when those who had received no advice were excluded.[17] Handicapped young people who were unemployed when interviewed were slightly less likely to have seen a careers officer (71 per cent, compared with 77 per cent of those working) and more likely to have seen a teacher other than a careers teacher (11 per cent compared with 5 per cent) or a relative or friend (11 per cent compared with 6 per cent). Differences in careers advice according to subsequent social class are brought out more clearly by distinguishing manual and non-manual groups. Nine out of ten of the non-manual group saw a careers officer compared with three-quarters of the manual group; whereas 17 per cent of the manual workers, compared with none of the non-manual workers, saw only a teacher.[18]

Among the handicapped groups, the physically handicapped were the most likely to have seen a careers officer or disablement resettlement officer (DRO) rather than less expert sources of advice, and the maladjusted were the least likely. Thus 81 per cent of the physically handicapped, 77 per cent of ESN(M) and 68 per cent of maladjusted young people had seen a careers officer. None of the former, and 7 per cent of the ESN(M), but a relatively large proportion of the maladjusted – 16 per cent – had seen only a relative or friend. Thus there were significant differences between the maladjusted and the non-handicapped young people.[19]

Careers Service

Those young people who had seen a careers officer were asked whether or not one of their parents had been with them. Three-fifths of both of the main sample groups said their parents had not been with them. Among the handicapped group, however, there were considerable (and in view of their different labour market experiences) important variations. Over half the physically handicapped had been accompanied by at least one parent, compared with one-third of maladjusted and one-quarter of ESN(M) young people.

Although overall only a small number of young people said that they had not heard of the Careers Service, this applied to one in ten of the handicapped compared with one in twenty-five of the non-handicapped. A further significant group (one-fifth of the handi-capped and one-sixth of the non-handicapped) had heard of the Careers Service but had never talked to a careers officer. Again, there were important differences amongst the handicapped: 14 per cent of the physically handicapped had not heard of the Careers Service or had not talked to a careers officer; compared with 29 per cent of ESN(M) and 45 per cent of maladjusted young people.[20]

Careers teaching in school

As well as having less contact than the non-handicapped with the Careers Service, handicapped young people were three times as likely at the age of 16, to have been in schools which did *not* have a careers teacher (45 per cent compared with 15 per cent). However, the proportion of non-handicapped young people who had not spoken to their careers teacher was more than twice that of the handicapped. So nearly two-thirds of the handicapped and over half the non-handicapped, people either had no careers teacher at their school or had not spoken to the careers teacher about their future. This applied to six out of ten of the physically handicapped and ESN(M), and seven out of ten of maladjusted young people.[21] In addition, as many as 70 per cent of the handicapped had *not* talked to another teacher about jobs or training before leaving school.

Handicapped young people were also slightly less likely to have had careers lessons in school (36 per cent compared with 48 per cent of the non-handicapped had had no careers lessons in school) and the physically handicapped and ESN(M) less than other groups. The maladjusted were least likely to have had *regular* careers lessons. The 'would benefit' group reported *regular* careers lessons most commonly (37 per cent), but only one-quarter of the handi-capped did so.[22]

Often practical experience is more useful than advice alone in giving young people a guide to working life (see Chapters 8 and 9). Seventy per cent of both handicapped and non-handicapped young people were likely to have had talks, visits and work experience. The non-handicapped were twice as likely as the handicapped to have had only talks and films about jobs and the handicapped were nearly three times as likely only to have been on visits. Among the handicapped 25 per cent of the ESN(M), 32 per cent of the physical-ly handicapped and 42 per cent of the maladjusted had had neither talks, films, work experience nor been on visits to factories or other work places. More than six out of ten of each sample group said they were not given advice on living and working in the adult world.[23]

Advice on leaving school

One of the most important decisions that young people have to make is whether to leave or stay on at school. In some instances, of course, there is no such choice; the young person may have to leave because the school will not allow him to stay on or strongly advises against it, or because his parents will not let him. The advice that young people receive at this important stage of their lives may have a significant impact on their later experience of work.

Young people in the survey were asked whether they had spoken to anyone about leaving or staying at school, and a hierarchy of expertise was constructed from their answers. (Again where a young person had spoken to more than one person, the most expert was counted). The handicapped were more than twice as likely as the non-handicapped not to have spoken to anyone about leaving school and less likely to have spoken to a careers officer or careers teacher. Non-handicapped young people were unlikely to have left school without receiving careers advice. Differences between the handicapped and non-handicapped were statistically very significant.[24]

Eighty per cent of those handicapped young people whose most informed adviser was a careers officer were working when interviewed, compared with 52 per cent of those who had received no advice about leaving school.

Careers education

Official and independent research studies have also demonstrated the low priority given to careers education in schools and the inconsistencies in practice between schools. The Department of Education and Science's (DES) survey of careers education in secondary schools in 1971 and 1972 concluded that 'The concept of careers education as that element in the school programme more especially concerned with preparation for living and working in the adult world is not at present generally accepted nor put into practice except by a minority of schools.'[25]

Although there had been some improvements since the earlier enquiry carried out for the Schools Council, which found that careers work in 50 per cent of schools was in the hands of teachers with no training in such work and a further 33 per cent where the teacher had received a maximum of two weeks' training,[26] the authors of the survey still expressed concern at the 'grave inadequacy' of careers teaching resources in schools. This pattern is confirmed by Kirton's research amongst sixth form boys.[27] Thomas and Wetherell found that two-fifths of boys attended secondary schools where there was no official careers work, while on the other hand, two-fifths received careers lessons as a regular part of the curriculum in their final year.[28]

The results of this study and those of the third NCDS follow-up indicate some improvement in the coverage of careers advice in schools since studies carried out in the early 1970s. For example, at the last NCDS follow-up nearly three-quarters of 16-year-olds were in schools where a teacher was paid a responsibility allowance for careers work.[29] However both surveys also confirm the wide differences between the careers guidance given to handicapped and to other young people in schools. At the age of sixteen only 2 per cent of all young people were in schools where there was no teacher responsible for careers work. But in special schools, some 34 per cent of pupils had no teacher responsible for careers guidance.[30] Although there are some outstanding examples of careers guidance and training and leavers' programmes in some special schools (for example, the pioneering work of Ann Hanson at the Ifield School in Gravesend),[31] handicapped young people appear to be receiving the least careers teaching in school, although their disadvantage in the labour market would suggest the need for extra help.

This finding is especially worrying when taken in conjunction with the suggestion in Chapter 9 that careers teaching was important in promoting stable employment histories. Furthermore, if as the data suggest, careers officers have greater contact with the handicapped who get the more skilled jobs, there is a pressing need for attention to be focussed on the most disadvantaged young people who receive the least advice and support.

Summary

This chapter considered the experience of the sample in the preparation for the transition from school to work. Similarly large proportions of both handicapped and non-handicapped young people received careers advice from a careers officer. Handicapped young people in skilled non-manual jobs were more likely than the less skilled to have seen a careers officer. The handicapped were more than twice as likely as the non-handicapped *not* to have heard of the Careers Service. In addition, they were three times as likely to have been in schools that did not have a careers teacher.

More than twice the proportion of handicapped young people as non-handicapped had not spoken to anyone about leaving school, and the latter were much more likely to have had 'expert' advice from a careers officer or careers teacher about leaving school. The non-handicapped were more likely than the handicapped to have got a job immediately after leaving school.

8

Employment and Underemployment

In this chapter the labour market experiences of the young people are examined in some depth. The first of the two main classifications of labour market experience developed for this research – the proportion of time in work – is used to assess and compare the achievements of the two main sample groups, and those of the different groups of handicapped young people, over their first two years in the labour market. Unless otherwise stated the analysis is based on the 'latest' job, that is the current job or if unemployed, the last job held. A summary of the main findings is provided at the end of the chapter.

Proportion of time in work

It was shown in Table 4.2 that 27 per cent of handicapped and 4 per cent of non-handicapped young people were unemployed, a ratio of nearly seven to one. Although this indicates a major social division in the burden of unemployment, it provides only a single snapshop picture of worklessness and may mask many different labour market experiences. Some of the individuals described in Chapter 3, such as Peter, Elaine and Sharon, could have appeared in official statistics as unemployed at some stage, but all three had very different early working careers. In order to begin to assess the qualitative differences in these experiences it is essential to measure employment and unemployment over a period of time. This reflects the fact that there is a continuum of labour market experiences stretching from continuous employment to continuous unemployment.

The first stage in assessing each young person's 'history' of employment and unemployment was to find out for how long they had been employed or unemployed. From the chronological record of work it was possible to calculate the total length of time in work and the total period without work. But, as the young people left school at different stages these totals were expressed as a proportion of the time available for work. This process involved the exclusion of those who had not worked (those in further education, training, borstal, hospital, adult training centres or still at school).

Table 8.1 shows the considerable difference in labour market experience between the handicapped and non-handicapped young people who had left school and reveals much more of the iceberg of disadvantage than does the current employment status. The differences between the four groups shown in table 8.1 are statistically very significant. If those young people not involved in further education or training were also included (for example, the severely handicapped in hospitals) the relative disadvantage of the handicapped would have been even greater.

TABLE 8.1 *Time spent in employment (%)*

Percentage of time spent in work	Sample group			
	Handi-capped	Special help	Would benefit	Non-handi-capped
None	2.0	3.4	(0.0)	2.9
One but less than 25	12.8	3.4	(6.2)	0.0
25 but less than 50	8.1	6.8	(2.1)	1.5
50 but less than 75	15.5	6.8	(12.5)	5.9
75 but less than 100	11.5	8.5	(8.3)	16.2
100	50.0	71.2	(70.8)	73.5
Total	100	100	100	100
Number	148	59	48	69

Comparison of 4 sample groups: $(10 - 25, 26 - 75, 76$ and above).
$X^2 = 35.9$, 10 degrees of freedom, $p < 0.01$.

In the ensuing analysis those young people who were employed for less than half the total time available for work since they left school are referred to as the *underemployed* and those employed for more than three-quarters of the time as *fully employed*. Since the cell numbers of the special help and would benefit groups were very small when sub-divided, they have been excluded. Furthermore, as so few of the non-handicapped were less than fully employed (five in all) they are usually excluded from the control group. Only 35 per cent of the maladjusted were found to be fully employed for their first two years in the labour market. This compared with 65 per cent of the physically handicapped and 64 per cent of the ESN(M). Physically handicapped young people, however, were more likely than those in other groups to be underemployed: 35 per cent compared with 22 per cent of either the maladjusted or the ESN(M).[1]

Social class and underemployment

The importance of social class in influencing individual's experience of work has already been demonstrated and it was not unexpected therefore, that class would have an important bearing on the proportion of time spent *in* work. The relationship between the class of the *first* job and the proportion of time in work was very significant for the handicapped group but not significant for the non-handicapped.[2] Handicapped young people who entered skilled manual employment were much more likely than their unskilled counterparts to be fully employed and far less likely to be underemployed. Three out of every four of the handicapped who were in skilled manual jobs were fully employed, compared with two in five of the unskilled. Similarly only 3 per cent of the former, compared with nearly 50 per cent of the latter, were underemployed.

In contrast to the relationship between the proportion of time in work and the class of the first job, the social class of the *latest* job was not significant for the handicapped but was for the non-handicapped.[3] Significant proportions of handicapped young people from all social classes were employed for less than the total time since leaving school, whereas among the non-handicapped those similarly employed were concentrated paradoxically in the *non-manual* classes. The key factor in this association was the difference in the employment records of young men and young women. Non-handicapped young women tended to hold their latest jobs in the non-manual work and also were more likely to be employed for less than the full period available (they are not referred to as underemployed because if they were not employed for the whole of the time since leaving school, they were likely to be unemployed for only relatively short periods (see Table 8.1).

Ninety-seven per cent of the non-handicapped whose latest jobs were in the skilled manual class were fully employed. The key influence here was the apprenticeship system, which had an important bearing on stability, at least in the short run. All of those in apprenticeships were fully employed. But, clearly, class was not the only significant factor. Even among the semi-skilled and unskilled non-handicapped, more than nine in ten were fully employed. Nearly nine out of ten of the underemployed handicapped young people had their latest jobs in the semi-skilled or unskilled classes and approximately two-fifths of them were unskilled.

So, there was a major social division between handicapped and non-handicapped young people in the distribution of underemployment and full employment. This division was also related to occupational class. I now turn to an examination of the interrelationship between the proportion of time in work and other aspects of employment and the search for work and, finally, personal characteristics.

Satisfaction with work

It was shown in Chapter 5 that the handicapped were more likely than other groups to be unhappy with their current or latest job. Here they have been shown to have formed the overwhelming majority of the underemployed. Analysis of the two variables together revealed that there was a significant association between proportion of time spent in work and job satisfaction[4] and that it was the underemployed handicapped young people who were most likely to be happy.

Within the handicapped group, 31 per cent of the underemployed were relatively *un*happy in work compared with 15 per cent of those fully employed. This trend is even clearer if attention is focused at the extremes – those employed for up to one-quarter of the total possible time and those employed for all the time since leaving school. The proportion of the latter who were very happy in work (42 per cent) was nearly twice that of the former. Similarly, while only 1 per cent of the fully employed were very unhappy, this applied to 18 per cent of those employed for no more than one-quarter of the time. None of the non-handicapped were very unhappy, but 86 per cent of those who were very happy were employed for all of the time since leaving school.

Entry into employment

There was a clear, consistent and very significant relationship between the young person's job situation immediately on leaving school and the proportion of time spent in work over the following two years.[5] The variables were, of course, partly related so that some association between them was not unexpected.

The figures for handicapped young people demonstrated the fundamental importance of a successful transition from school to employment: 57 per cent of those who got a job immediately after leaving school were still employed and only 5 per cent were employed for less than one-quarter of their available time. On the other hand, 41 per cent of those who had been unemployed or sick straight after leaving school were in work for less than 25 per cent of the time, and 28 per cent of them were fully employed. Furthermore, the longer that handicapped young people were out of work after leaving school the less likely they were to enter secure employment. Thus, nearly two-thirds of those who were sick or unemployed for three months or more after leaving school, were finally employed for a maximum of only a quarter of their time. A smaller proportion (one-fifth) of those unemployed for less than three months after leaving school were employed under a quarter of the time.

Nearly nine out of ten of the fully employed handicapped people got a job at once, which in the majority of cases, meant that they had fixed up a job before leaving school. Of those handicapped young people employed for a quarter or less of their time, fewer than one-third got work immediately. Most of the non-handicapped who had left school went straight into employment, and over three-quarters of these were employed for all the time since leaving school.

There was strong evidence, therefore, that if the young person went straight from school into work there was a great probability that at best he or she would stay, or that at least he or she would be successful again in getting subsequent jobs. This important relationship between the entry into employment and the proportion of time spent in work, underlines the points made briefly in Chapter 7 about the need for sound advice and guidance before leaving school, and suggests an important role for measures to ease the transition from school to work for handicapped young people in particular.

Number of jobs

There was a very significant relationship within the handicapped group between the proportion of time spent in work and the number of jobs held.[6] It was surprising that similar proportions of underemployed and fully employed handicapped young people had held one (55 per cent compared with 52 per cent), two (19 per cent and 20 per cent), three (10 per cent and 14 per cent), four (10 per cent) and five or more jobs (6 per cent and 4 per cent). But this similarity was caused by very different early labour market careers.

First, the majority of the underemployed held one or two jobs for brief periods but had spent most of the two years unemployed. Secondly, this contrasted with the fully employed, most of whom had held one or two jobs, but had spent very little time out of work. In between these two extremes there was a third (and very different) type of labour market career. This group of handicapped young people had held two or more jobs for periods usually totalling between one year and 18 months, and were unemployed for the remaining period.

The majority of the non-handicapped held no more than two jobs and had spent very little time out of work. In contrast to the underemployed handicapped young people, the non-handicapped who had had more than two jobs moved quickly from one to another.

Since a large proportion of the underemployed handicapped had held only one or two jobs the question arose as to why they had left these jobs and become unemployed. The reasons given by young people for leaving their *first* job revealed important differences between the underemployed and the fully employed. The proportion of the underemployed who were sacked from their first job was nearly twice that for the fully employed. Moreover, the former were twice as likely as the latter to leave for financial reasons and four times as likely to leave to get married or for health reasons.[7]

Thirty-seven per cent of the underemployed handicapped young people left their first (and for the majority their only) job, for reasons which may have been largely beyond their control (that is, they were sacked, made redundant, deemed not to have met requirements, were in poor health, or the work was temporary). This figure compares unfavourably with 30 per cent for the fully employed and 30 per cent for fully employed non-handicapped young people. In addition, over half the latter consisted of young people who had done temporary work, either as a prelude to a training or education course, or a better job, or in a planned way, such as temporary secretarial work. In other words, they had socially legitimate reasons for leaving those jobs.

The pattern of the three types of labour market career outlined above was reinforced by differences in the reasons given by handicapped young people for leaving their first job. The underemployed were more likely than the fully employed to have had to leave their first jobs. But they were also more likely to have left for their own reasons. They were four times as likely to get married or have a baby, twice as likely to leave for more money and one and a half times as likely to leave because they did not like the job. This difference between the underemployed and those fully employed was largely attributable to the significant proportion of the latter who had had only one job. If this group were excluded, the proportions leaving for different reasons were very similar, with three notable exceptions: the underemployed remained more likely than the fully employed to leave for health reasons, or to have a baby, and less likely to have left because their job was only temporary. The difference between the fully employed and the third, intermediate, group (those employed for between half and three-quarters of the time since leaving school) was also clear. Similar proportions were sacked, made redundant or did not like the work; over twice the proportion of the intermediate group left for family reasons; nearly twice as many for financial or health reasons and the proportion who left because they had been doing only temporary work was three times less than that for the fully employed. In fact there were greater similarities in the reasons given for leaving their first job, between the group of underemployed and those employed for between half and three-quarters of their time since leaving school. This is not surprising because *both* groups may be classed as 'relatively' underemployed, although the labour market careers contributing to this similarity were quite different.

Aspirations and attitudes towards work

There were important differences between the underemployed and fully employed in their aspirations. Those handicapped young people who did *not* aspire to jobs other than their current one were most likely to be employed for a high proportion of time – 18 per cent of the fully employed, compared with 6 per cent of the underemployed. More significantly, the proportion of the under-employed who aspired to non-manual jobs (27 per cent) was twice the average for the whole handicapped group and one and a half times that for the non-handicapped. So if there were 'unreasonably' high aspirations throughout the handicapped (see Chapter 6) they were concentrated in the underemployed group.[8] However, scrutiny of the *type* of ideal job to which they aspired showed that while 13 per cent of the underemployed aspired to professional or intermediate jobs compared with 8 per cent of the fully employed handicapped and 22 per cent of the non-handicapped (almost equal proportions of these groups aspired to service sector jobs), the main difference was that over twice the proportion of the underemployed as other groups, wanted *clerical* rather than higher status jobs.[9]

Differences in the proportion of time spent in work by handicapped young people were affected by their different orientation towards work. One in three of the underemployed had an extrinsic orientation, compared with just under one in four of the fully employed. One in six of the underemployed compared with one in three of the fully employed, held career orientations.[10]

Careers teaching

Was the proportion of time the young people spent in work over the two years influenced by the careers advice they had received prior to leaving school and during the transition from school to work, or by the information and help they received on entering the labour market?

There was no significant difference between underemployed and fully employed handicapped young people in the extent of their contact with a careers teacher.[11] There was similarly no difference between those from schools with and without a teacher who was paid a special salary for giving careers guidance.[12] Again there was little overall difference between the two groups of handicapped young people in whether they had had careers lessons at school: three-fifths of both the under and fully employed had received none. However there were differences at the extremes: 73 per cent of those employed for no more than one-quarter of the time had had no careers lessons, while 53 per cent of those employed for the total time had received none.[13]

If talking to careers teachers or other teachers did not prove significant in dividing young people, more practical experience and information from *outside* the school had some bearing on the proportion of time spent in work. Young people were asked whether they had had any talks or films in school about jobs apart from careers lessons, and also whether they had ever visited factories or offices, had talks from working people about work or taken part in a work experience scheme. Two-fifths of underemployed handicapped young people had none of these practical careers lessons compared with one-fifth of the fully employed. In addition there was a similar, significant difference between the fully employed and less than fully employed non-handicapped young people in the receipt of these careers lessons.[14]

Careers advice and guidance

There appeared to be no relationship between contact with the Careers Service and the length of time handicapped young people spent in work. Similar proportions of underemployed and fully employed handicapped young people had one, two, three or more talks with the careers officer. However, 18 per cent of the former compared with 7 per cent of the latter said that they had never heard of the careers officer.

Young people were asked about their interview with the careers officer and in particular about the jobs *they* had mentioned to him. A pattern of differences between the underemployed and fully employed could be discerned from an examination of the *types* of job young people proposed to the careers officer. Differences were most apparent at the extremes. Thirty-six per cent of those employed for no more than one-quarter of the time since leaving school mentioned artistic or professional work, perhaps the most difficult jobs to obtain, compared with only 2 per cent of those employed for the whole period. The majority of the latter proposed service or industrial manual work (57 per cent).[16]

So it would appear that the lower the level of the job first proposed by the handicapped young person to the careers officer (perhaps the more realistic choice), the greater the likelihood of success in achieving relatively secure employment. However, if their ambitions were 'unreasonable' *prior* to labour market entry, they were soon altered after leaving school (see Table 6.3). It was difficult to account for the association between the type of employment proposed to a careers officer and the proportion of time spent in work. Young people may have been less successful when their ambitions were thwarted; the Careers Service may be more efficient at placing young people in low-skill jobs and may reject higher aspirations. On the other hand if young people hold ambitions that are unrealistic in a given labour market and opportunity structure, this may jeopardise their chances of a successful transition from school to work, a key aspect in ensuring subsequent steady employment.

Information about jobs

Young people were asked how they had heard about each job they had held. Parents were at least as successful as official channels as a source of information about jobs resulting in secure employment. The majority of handicapped young people who had heard about their latest job through their parents (68 per cent) were employed for the whole period since leaving school. This also applied to two-thirds of those who had heard about their job from their teacher or other teacher, just over one-half of those who had heard from a careers officer, one-half who had heard from a social worker, disablement resettlement officer or as a result of temporary work, and only 17 per cent of those who used a Jobcentre (though of course the latter agencies would be more likely to be contacted by those who had been unemployed).[17]

Differences in the type of work experience of the handicapped young people who were underemployed and fully employed were further illustrated by the agencies that they nominated as being the best way of finding work. Thus the underemployed were four times as likely as the fully employed to mention the Department of Employment or Jobcentre (48 per cent did so) and nearly three times *less* likely to have mentioned either friends or relatives or the Careers Service (8 per cent and 8 per cent).[18] These differences were very significant. A contrast between the two extreme groups, those employed for no more than one-quarter of the total possible time and those employed for the whole period since leaving school, emphasised the relative importance of the Careers Service to the fully employed and the Jobcentres to the underemployed. Thus 13 per cent of the former, compared with 25 per cent of the latter, nominated the Careers Service, while 53 per cent compared with 9 per cent, said that the Department of Employment was the best way of finding work.

Gender and functional capacity[19]

There was a very significant association between the sex of the individual and the proportion of time spent in work.[20] Women were much more likely to be underemployed than men (32 per cent compared with 18 per cent) and much less likely to have been fully employed (54 per cent compared with 66 per cent). This difference was widest amongst the least employed handicapped group where only one in ten young men were employed for no more than one-quarter of the total possible time compared with nearly one in four females. This sexual difference also applied to the non-handicapped: 72 per cent of those employed for the whole post-school period were male.

TABLE 8.2 *Employment capacity and time spent in work (%)*

	Proportion of time in work			
Degree of incapacity	Up to 50%	50 to 75%	Over 75%	Total
None	(20.6)	(34.8)	40.7	35.1
Some	(79.4)	(65.2)	59.3	64.9
Total	100	100	100	100
Number	34	23	91	148

$X^2 = 47.3$, 1 degree of freedom, $p < 0.001$.

Table 8.2 shows the analysis of fully and underemployed according to the severity of the handicap. Handicapped young people who were assessed as appreciably, severely or very severely handicapped by the capacity of employment index are not included because they had not worked since leaving school. These handicapped young people were predominantly ESN(S) and some were physically handicapped. Thus, the very significant correlation between proportion of time in work and this index, was higher than that shown in the table. Because of the exclusion of the most severely handicapped, the remainder, classified as slightly or moderately handicapped, have been combined. Differences between the underemployed and fully employed on the self-care index were not statistically significant. There were only slight differences between the underemployed and fully employed on the third index of functional capacity (social communication and participation).

Data from the first NCDS follow-up showed that those handicapped young people who were underemployed between the ages of 16 and 18, were more likely than the fully employed to have been classified by doctors as mentally retarded at 7 years and much more likely to be more than slightly handicapped. Because of the absence of data from previous NCDS follow-ups and the reduced numbers which result from this, the term 'underemployed' from now on will be used to refer to those young people who are employed for no more than three-quarters of the total possible time. Three-fifths of the underemployed, compared with three-quarters of the fully employed had no mental retardation at 7 years; 12 per cent compared with 13 per cent had a slight mental handicap and 22 per cent compared with only 6 per cent were moderately handicapped. These differences were statistically significant despite the exclusion of the severely mentally handicapped young people (ESN(S)), who had not worked in open employment.[21]

Educational ability and schooling

Analysis of data from the NCDS educational questionnaire suggested a tendency for those who had been receiving special help in school for educational or mental backwardness when they were 16, to be underemployed. Sixty-eight per cent of those employed for up to three-quarters of the time since leaving school had received such special help at the age of 16, compared with 55 per cent of the fully employed. A further 20 per cent of the former needed more help, compared with 12 per cent of the latter; while 12 per cent and 32 per cent respectively were not receiving any help for educational or mental backwardness.[22] Fully employed handicapped young people were slightly *more* likely than the underemployed to have been in remedial classes and were slightly *less* likely to have been in special schools.[23] One in every eight of the fully employed (for whom there was data) were in remedial classes compared with none of the underemployed; and 51 per cent and 68 per cent were in special schools.[24]

Parental interest in education

At the third NCDS follow-up, teachers were asked whether the parents of each child studied were interested in that child's education. Handicapped young people whose parents were over-concerned, very interested or who showed some interest were less likely than those whose parents showed little or no apparent interest to be underemployed, and were more likely to be fully employed.[25] Nineteen per cent of the former compared with 29 per cent of the latter were underemployed, and 72 per cent compared with 55 per cent were fully employed. Only 8 per cent of the parents of those who were employed for no more than one-quarter of the possible time were very interested in their child's education, according to teachers, while 54 per cent showed little interest. These results were not statistically significant.

Parents' social class and home environment

Data collected at the third NCDS follow-up indicated that the fathers of less than fully employed handicapped young people were chiefly in the skilled manual (54 per cent), semi-skilled (15 per cent) and unskilled (23 per cent) classes. (Again, the definition of under-employment has been modified slightly to include all those working for three-quarters or less of the time since leaving school). Fathers of the fully employed were also predominantly from the skilled manual (46 per cent) and semi-skilled manual classes (25 per cent) but 19 per cent were from the professional and intermediate classes.[26]

The less than fully-employed were more likely than the fully employed to be living in overcrowded accommodation at the age of 16.[27] Of those handicapped 16-year-olds in accommodation with up to 1.5 persons per room (one of the standard definitions of overcrowding) 32 per cent were subsequently less than fully employed compared with 55 per cent of the overcrowded. Only three of the non-handicapped (for whom there was NCDS data) were in overcrowded accommodation at the age of 16.

There was also some indication, but the numbers are too small to be significant, that those handicapped young people without the sole use of basic amenities such as a bath or toilet at the age of 16 were more likely than others with such amenities, to be underemployed.[28] Underemployed handicapped young people were slightly more likely than the fully employed to have been in council accommodation at age 11 (68 per cent and 56 per cent) and less likely to be in owner-occupied housing (18 per cent compared with 28 per cent).[29] One-half of handicapped young people who were living in council houses or flats at the age of 11 were employed for the whole of the post-school period, compared with 71 per cent of those in owner-occupied houses. Furthermore, 18 per cent of the former compared with 3 per cent of the latter were employed for one-quarter or less of the time since leaving school. Underemployed handicapped young people were more likely than the fully employed to have left home or to live in either a single or large family household.

Summary

The proportion of the handicapped who had spent less than half their time actually in work – the underemployed – was *five* times that of the non-handicapped. At the other extreme six out of ten of the handicapped compared with nine out of ten of the non-handicapped had been employed for more than three-quarters of the time since leaving. Nearly nine out of ten underemployed handicapped young people were semi-skilled or unskilled. A large proportion of non-handicapped young people who had not been out of work since leaving school were in engineering jobs, mainly apprenticeships.

Careers advice from careers teachers and other teachers had very little relation to labour market achievements. There was some indication that careers lessons were influential. In particular the more practical forms of careers guidance, such as work experience and visits to factories were associated with success in the labour market. But overall the role of careers guidance was minimal. Those young people who were unemployed straight after leaving school were out of work longest in the two years. Nearly three-fifths of the handicapped who got jobs immediately after leaving school were fully employed. Among the fully employed handicapped *and* non-handicapped, individual and parental initiative were significant factors in finding the young person's first job. Those handicapped young people who proposed semi-skilled jobs in their interview with the careers officer were the most successful in getting and keeping work.

The underemployed had more often than the fully employed been classified as mentally retarded when aged 7, and were nearly four times as likely to have been moderately retarded. Fathers of the underemployed handicapped young people were predominately in manual social classes. They were nearly four times as likely to be unskilled as parents of the fully employed and three times less likely to be in the professional or intermediate classes. The underemployed were more likely than the fully employed to be living in overcrowded accommodation when they were 16.

9

Job Stability and Subemployment

In this chapter the results of applying the second classification of labour market experiences – job stability – are presented and its relation to a wide range of data is discussed in an attempt to distinguish between relatively successful and unsuccessful early labour market careers. Data on the young people's incomes are also examined and finally, the concepts of job stability and subemployment are discussed briefly as a prelude to the analysis of employers and training in the next two chapters.

Stability of employment history

Although there has been much research into the attitudes of adolescents and the conditions they meet when entering employment,[1] there is little information on the forms that early labour market histories take. It is generally agreed that young people change their jobs more frequently than adults. As Carter notes: 'There are not national figures giving the precise extent of job changing amongst the workers, but research studies suggest that a substantial proportion of 15-year-old leavers change jobs during their first few years at work, many of them several times.'[2]

Handicapped young people in this study changed their jobs more frequently than the non-handicapped, and women more than men. The average number of jobs per handicapped young person was 2.4 compared with 1.7 for the non-handicapped. But nearly one in four of the former compared with one in ten of the latter had held four or more jobs.[3] Ferguson and Cunnison found that nearly half of the 1 300 boys they studied in Glasgow had held at least three jobs in as many years, and 14 per cent had held five or more.[4] Sixteen per cent of secondary modern school-leavers, of both sexes, studied by the Crowther Committee, had held four or more jobs in the first three years after leaving school.[5]

Job stability index

Statistics such as these, however, reveal only part of the young persons' early labour market experience. Examination of the proportion of time young people actually spent in work went beyond the snapshot picture provided by current employment status and showed the full impact of unemployment on the school-leaver. Similarly with the nature of each young person's employment record: the number of jobs indicates the frequency of job-turnover, but this must be seen in the context of the total time available for work. Furthermore, frequency of job-turnover does not give any indication of the amount of time actually spent in work.

In previous research on unemployment by Hill and Daniel the *number of spells* of unemployment was used as a key indicator.[6] But this may tell us very little about employment experiences over a period of time or about the exact impact of unemployment. For example it may be argued that young people can be expected to change jobs frequently as a kind of settling down process. But by looking at the proportion of time spent in work we can determine the extent to which this 'settling-in process' is a rapid adjustment to, say, changing opportunities or personal job tastes, or a process that is dominated by unemployment, interspersed with relatively short spells of employment. In other words, what is of crucial importance, is the length of time the young person spent out of work *between* jobs. Thus the proportion of time spent in employment was combined with the number of jobs to form an *index of job stability*.

Only those young people who had entered employment were included and the following three groups were distinguished on the basis of: the number of jobs that they had entered, the time available to them since leaving school and the length of time in and out of work:

(i)   *Very stable work history.* Those who had held one or two jobs in two years (with different firms) and had been in work for 21 months; one job in 18 months and in work for 15 months or more; and one job in one year and in work for 9 months or more.

(ii)   *Very unstable work history.* Those who had held four or more jobs in two years or had been in work for less than six months; three or more jobs in 18 months or in work for less than six months; two or more jobs in one year or in work for less than three months, or continuously unemployed.

(iii)   *Stable work history*. The group remaining from (i) and (ii).

Table 9.1 shows that handicapped young people were more than twice as likely as the non-handicapped to have very unstable employment records. These differences were statistically very significant.

TABLE 9.1 *Stability of employment (%)*[a]

| Employment history | Sample group | | | | |
	Handi-capped	Special help	Would benefit	Non-handi-capped	Total at 18[b]
Very stable	35.8	57.1	(58.3)	69.6	65.4
Stable	27.1	14.3	(18.7)	16.1	15.9
Very unstable	35.8	26.8	(20.8)	14.3	15.1
Insufficient information	1.3	1.8	(2.1)	0.0	3.6
Total	100	100	100	100	100
Number	151	56	48	56	16 950

[a] Excludes those who had not worked.
[b] Rough estimate for all 18-year-olds based on the total numbers in the NCDS cohort at 16.
Handicapped *vs* non-handicapped: $X^2 = 24.0$, 6 degrees of freedom, $p < 0.001$.

Within the handicapped group, the physically handicapped had the most stable employment records and the maladjusted the least stable. Forty-one per cent of the physically handicapped were very stable and 29 per cent unstable. Thirty-five per cent of the ESN(M) were very stable and 40 per cent very unstable; and 25 per cent of the maladjusted were very stable and 42 per cent unstable.[7]

Number of jobs

Job stability was partly defined by the number of jobs held. Handicapped young people with very stable employment histories had all held only one or two jobs, and those with stable histories one, two or three jobs (55 per cent of the latter had held three jobs). Many of the young people in these groups corresponded to the fully employed group distinguished in the previous chapter. But the very unstable divided naturally into two groups: those with long periods of unemployment and those with a relatively large number of jobs. The former were largely underemployed. Thus one-third of the very unstable had held only one or two jobs but had long periods of unemployment. The second, larger group had held more jobs than the majority of the underemployed and had experienced less unemployment. Thus 60 per cent of the very unstable had held four or more jobs and 17 per cent six or more jobs.[8] It was the maladjusted and ESN(M) young people who were most likely to have held a relatively large number of jobs.

There were considerable differences between those 18-year-olds with stable and unstable employment records in the reasons they gave for leaving their first job (when a job change had been made). These, in turn, reflected differences in type of employment and attitudes towards work. Two-thirds of those with very stable employment records had held only one job. The proportion of the very unstable who were sacked or made redundant was more than twice that of the very stable. Furthermore, 14 per cent compared with 37 per cent left because they did not like some aspect of the job (the most common reason), over five times as many left because of low pay and three times as many because of ill-health.[9]

Those handicapped young people who left their first job for personal reasons, for example, because they wanted more money, as opposed to 'unavoidable' reasons such as being sacked or ill-health, showed significantly more unstable work histories: 54 per cent of the former and 42 per cent of the latter.[10] Amongst the non-handicapped there was little instability. What little there was, was often attributable to the temporary nature of their employment.

Type of work and social class

What kind of work did those with stable and unstable work histories do? Handicapped young people in engineering jobs, farming and agricultural work showed twice as many very stable as very unstable employment records. Those doing clerical work were also more often stable than unstable. This trend was reversed in only two occupational groupings: industrial manual work and building.[11]

The non-handicapped control group most closely approximated to the general population of 18-year-olds (see Chapter 2) and their experience indicated the types of work which might have encouraged stable employment histories amongst all young people. Over half of those in the service sector, three-quarters in clerical work and nine out of ten in engineering (mainly apprenticeships) were relatively stable. One in three of the non-handicapped in industrial manual work and one in four in the building sector had unstable work histories. But the handicapped in industrial and building jobs were more likely than the non-handicapped in similar types of work to be unstable.

It was, yet again, when we turned to analyse social class (based on the young person's occupation – see Chapter 4) that important differences within the handicapped group were explained. The differences shown in Table 9.2 were statistically very significant.

TABLE 9.2 *Stability of employment and social class (%)*

Social class[a]	Type of employment record			Total
	Very stable	Stable	Very unstable	
Skilled non-manual	12.7	(6.8)	3.4	8.1
Skilled manual	25.4	(18.2)	13.8	19.2
Semi-skilled	47.3	(54.5)	41.4	46.0
Unskilled	14.5	(20.4)	34.5	24.2
Unclassifiable	0.0	(0.0)	1.7	0.6
Continuously unemployed	0.0	0.0	5.2	1.9
Total	100	100	100	100
Number	55	44	58	157

[a] based on current or last job.

$X^2 = 20.7$, 3 degrees of freedom, $p < 0.001$.

Important differences between handicapped young people can be illustrated by contrasting the highest and lowest social classes in which they are found. Fifty-four per cent of the skilled non-manual group were very stable and only 15 per cent were very unstable. At the other extreme the position was reversed with only 20 per cent of the unskilled having stable, and 51 per cent having very unstable, employment histories.

Entry into employment

A comparison between handicapped young people with very stable and very unstable work histories illustrates the importance of a successful transition from school to work. Those young people who went straight from school into work were very significantly more likely to have stable employment records.[12] Nine out of ten of those with stable records compared with just over six out of ten of those with unstable records went straight from school into work. Of those who were unemployed for up to three months, the ratio of 'unstable' to 'stable' was two to one. None of the very stable were unemployed for more than three months, compared with one in seven of the unstable.

Unused capacity

An attempt was made to secure subjective assessments of unused capacity by asking young people if they felt that they were doing less than they could. There was a very significant relationship between employment record and this unused capacity.[13] Seventy per cent of the very stable compared with 40 per cent of the very unstable said they were *not* underusing their abilities, while 26 per cent compared with 36 per cent thought they had unused capacity. Physically handicapped young people were most likely to say they had unused capacity: (58 per cent compared with 31 per cent of the ESN(M) and 25 per cent of the maladjusted).[14]

Job training

There was a very important and statistically significant relationship between job training and stability of employment history.[15] Those handicapped young people whose latest jobs contained an element of training beyond simply being shown what to do, were more likely to have stable employment records. This finding is, of course, linked to the relationship between social class (or skill level) and stability. Two-thirds of handicapped young people with very unstable work histories had received training on the job for one day or less, or no training at all, compared with just over one-third of the very stable. None of those in apprenticeships or on day-release courses had very unstable employment records.

Other employment factors

There were very significant differences between those handicapped young people with stable and unstable work histories in their perceptions of their experience in comparison with others.[16] The 18-year-olds were asked how they felt that their first two years at work had compared with those of other young people. Forty-five per cent of the very stable thought that they had done better, and 4 per cent worse, than average, while for the unstable the trend was reversed – 11 per cent felt that they had done better, and 33 per cent worse, than average.

It was shown in Chapter 5 that handicapped young people were less happy in work than others. But within the handicapped group it was the less successful – the underemployed and unstable – who were most unhappy. Handicapped young people with very stable employment records were seldom unhappy, and were much more likely than the unstable to be relatively happy. These differences among handicapped young people were statistically very significant.[17] Only 2 per cent of very stable handicapped young people were unhappy in their latest or current job compared with 13 per cent of those with unstable records; 43 per cent and 25 per cent respectively were very happy. Handicapped young people with very stable employment records were more likely than the unstable to be in higher social classes.[18] They were also, perhaps not surprisingly, more likely than the unstable *not* to aspire to jobs in a different social class. Fifty-seven per cent of the former compared with 74 per cent of the latter aspired to ideal jobs in different social classes.[19]

Careers advice and job information

Analysis of careers advice and job-search variables revealed a similar pattern to that shown by the previous analysis of the proportion of time spent in work. More handicapped young people with very stable job histories had had careers lessons in school than those with very unstable histories (51 per cent compared with 29 per cent).[20] A greater proportion of handicapped young people with very *un*stable work records had *not* consulted a careers officer at least once (40 per cent compared with 21 per cent of the very stable).[21]

There was a very significant association between contact with careers teachers at school and job stability.[22] More of the young people in each sample group with very stable employment histories had had a careers teacher in their school when they were 16, and had talked to him about their future. Forty-six per cent of very stable handicapped young people had no careers teacher at school or had not talked to one, compared with 64 per cent of the very unstable; 54 per cent and 36 per cent respectively had at least one talk with a careers teacher.

There was a very significant difference between handicapped young people with very stable and unstable employment records in the agencies they nominated as being the 'best way of finding work'.[23] Differences between the two groups were most marked in their reference to official agencies. Thus 26 per cent of those with very stable records nominated the Careers Service compared with 8 per cent of the very unstable. But on the other hand, 8 per cent compared with 34 per cent said that Jobcentres were the best places to find work. This lends support to previous findings suggesting that those with very stable employment records were most likely to have found jobs either at school or soon after leaving school. Those with very unstable work records appeared to pass quickly from the initial placement service of the Careers Service to the adult placement agencies.

Gender and functional capacity[24]

There was a slight tendency for the men to have more stable employment records than the women. Although similar proportions of handicapped young men and women had very stable employment records (35 per cent and 33 per cent) the women were more likely to be very unstable (46 per cent compared with 30 per cent of young men). While the majority of the non-handicapped were very stable, 12 per cent of the men and 23 per cent of the women were very unstable.[25]

As Table 9.3 shows, handicapped young people with very unstable employment histories were significantly more likely than the very stable to be handicapped according to the three scales of functional assessment. The most severely handicapped young people had not worked in open employment at all and therefore were not included in the table.

TABLE 9.3 *Stability of employment and functional capacity (%)*

Index	Degree of incapacity	Type of employment record			Total
		Very stable	Stable	Very unstable	
Self-care	none	94.4	(86.4)	75.9	84.7
	some	5.6	(13.6)	24.6	15.3
	total	100	100	100	100
Social communication	none	41.8	(56.8)	29.3	40.4
	some	58.2	(43.2)	70.7	59.6
	total	100	100	100	100
Employment	none	47.3	(34.1)	22.4	34.2
	some	52.7	(69.9)	77.6	65.8
	total	100	100	100	100
Number		55	44	58	157

Comparison of 3 types of employment record:
self-care: $X^2 = 8.0$, 2 degrees of freedom, $p < 0.05$
social communication: $X^2 = 7.8$, 2 degrees of freedom, $p < 0.05$
employment: $X^2 = 7.73$, 2 degrees of freedom, $p < 0.05$.

Psychological and mental handicaps

As well as a close correlation between functional incapacity and job stability there was a very significant association between the existence of minor nervous complaints and job stability.[26] All the young people were asked if they were troubled by certain personal problems, such as sleeping badly, loss of appetite, frequent headaches and getting into a rage with other people, which taken together might have indicated the presence of a minor nervous complaint. Amongst the handicapped with very stable employment histories 75 per cent had no nervous problems and 8 per cent had two or more. For the unstable the figures were 45 per cent with no nervous problems and 34 per cent with two or more. This relationship was constant for all sample groups: those with very stable employment records were unlikely to be troubled by such problems.

It was possible that there was a two-way causal relationship here. Because of the concentration of ESN(M) and maladjusted young people amongst those with unstable work histories the presence of some minor nervous complaints was expected. But there is also the psychological influence that instability and unemployment have on the young person as well as such complaints.[27] The correlation of these problems with instability across the sample groups indicates that they were not confined to those classified as 'handicapped'.

Handicapped young people with very unstable employment histories had more often than the very stable been assessed as moderately or severely mentally retarded at 7 years (16 per cent compared with 9 per cent) and were only slightly less likely not to be mentally retarded (61 per cent compared with 64 per cent). But the very stable were three times as likely as the unstable to have been only slightly mentally retarded at age 7.[28]

Special education

Handicapped young people with very stable employment histories were less likely than the very unstable to have received special help at school for mental or educational backwardness. They were more likely *not* to have needed such help. Thus 67 per cent of the very stable received such help at the age of 16 compared with 83 per cent of the very unstable; and 24 per cent compared with 15 per cent were not considered by their teachers to need such help.[29]

Differences between those receiving and not receiving special help for *behavioural* difficulties when they were 16 were even wider than those shown for other forms of help.[30] Thus 21 per cent of the handicapped with very stable employment histories, for whom there was NCDS data available, had been receiving such help at 16, compared with 50 per cent of the very unstable. Furthermore, teachers considered that 74 per cent of the former and only 41 per cent of the latter did not need such help.

Handicapped young people with very stable employment histories had (more often than the very unstable) attended an ordinary school and were much less likely to have been at a residential school for ESN pupils. Forty-one per cent of the former and 28 per cent of the latter were attending a comprehensive or secondary modern school when they were 16, whilst 4 per cent and 16 per cent respectively had attended a residential school for ESN pupils.[31]

Parental social class and home environment

As with underemployment, handicapped young people with very unstable employment histories were less likely than the very stable, to be the children of fathers in the higher social classes and were more likely to have fathers who were in the unskilled class. Twenty-three per cent of the fathers of the very stable handicapped were in the professional, intermediate or skilled non-manual classes compared with 6 per cent of the fathers of the very unstable. On the other hand, 8 per cent compared with 24 per cent respectively were in the unskilled class.[32]

Again, there was a significant relationship between housing tenure and job stability.[33] One in three handicapped young people with very stable employment histories were living in owner-occupied houses when they were 11 years old compared with less than one in five of the very unstable (18 per cent). Fifty-three per cent of the former and 61 per cent of the latter were in council accommodation at the age of 11 years.

Income

Apart from the social level and type of employment, individual's achievements are usually judged as successful or otherwise on the basis of material possessions. We live in a materialistic society and it is the level of income, as well as the possession of other visible resources by which people are often classified by others. Level of income is, of course, highly dependent on being in work and on the type of employment, and is analysed separately here as one reflection of the status and other achievements of young people in the sample. Detailed information was sought on *all* sources of income. Table 9.4 shows the financial status of the sample.

When those young people with no income or very small amounts of pocket-money were excluded (most of them were still at school), the difference between the handicapped and non-handicapped, at both ends of the income distribution was wide. The inclusion of the ESN(S) young people increased this difference at the lower end of the income scale. This severely handicapped group received their income predominantly from state sources. Over 70 per cent had incomes of under £20 per week. Even larger proportions of the physically handicapped had low incomes with three-quarters under £20 and nearly one-half under £15. Forty-eight per cent of the ESN(M) and 61 per cent of the maladjusted had weekly incomes of less than £20 net; 36 per cent and 46 per cent had weekly incomes of under £15.[34]

TABLE 9.4 *Income (%)*

Income[a] (£)	Sample groups			
	Handicapped[b]	Special help	Would benefit	Non-handi-capped
None	2.1	4.7	(6.1)	19.6
Less than 10	11.4 (14.0)	3.1	(4.1)	3.1
10–14	26.4 (24.9)	15.6	(12.2)	6.2
15–19	16.6 (18.3)	15.6	(18.4)	12.4
20–24	21.2 (20.5)	20.3	(18.4)	21.6
25–29	10.9 (10.0)	15.6	(18.4)	23.7
30–39	8.8 (8.8)	18.7	(18.4)	13.4
40 or more	2.6 (3.1)	6.2	(4.1)	1.0
Total	100 100	100	100	100
Number	193 229	64	49	97

[a] Last time paid (net)
[b] ESN(S) included in brackets
Handicapped *vs* non-handicapped: income grouped £0 – 10, 11 – 19, 20 – 29, 30+.
$X^2 = 19.7$, 3 degrees of freedom, $p < 0.001$.

It is helpful to judge these income levels against two relative standards. First, average earnings (gross): in October 1976 the average weekly earnings of men under 21 working full-time in all industries was £37.94 and for women under 18 years of age, working full-time £26.70. For all men aged 21 and over in full-time work the average was £66.97. Secondly, the supplementary benefit level which is often referred to as the official poverty line: at the time of the survey the ordinary level of supplementary benefit for a single person was £10.90 per week (plus the full amount of rent and rates) and this was raised to £12.70 (plus rent) in November 1976. Young people still living at home would not receive the full single householder's rate of £10.90 but the non-householder's rate of £8.70.

There were differences in income levels between the sexes, with women in general having lower incomes than men. For example, 16 per cent of ESN(M) women compared with 31 per cent of ESN(M) men had net weekly incomes of £25 or more. The figures for the non-handicapped were: 28 per cent of women and 48 per cent of men with this income.[35]

Level of income was, of course, related to source of income. So 99 per cent of handicapped young people with net incomes of £20 or more received their income solely from wages or salary. One in three of those with incomes under £20 received their income from this source, and slightly more than one in three received supplementary benefit. Among the non-handicapped, all those with incomes over £20 relied solely on wages or salary.[36]

There were also considerable inequalities between the main sample groups in the level of savings they had accrued by the age of 18. Just over one-half of the handicapped had no savings, compared with one-fifth of the non-handicapped. At the other extreme, 8 per cent of the former compared with 24 per cent of the latter had savings of £200 or more. So in terms of financial success, the first two years that the handicapped spent in the labour market were characterised by relatively low incomes, often because of unemployment and low state benefits and very small savings, while the non-handicapped who had worked more often, received higher incomes, usually from employment, and had more capital.[37]

Subemployment and the dual labour market

There was a very close relationship between income and the two main variables used to classify labour market experiences. For example, 88 per cent of underemployed handicapped young people had net weekly incomes of less than £20 (19 per cent had less than £10). This compared with just over one-quarter of the fully employed of whom 1 per cent had under £10.[38]

Turning to job stability, there were major and very significant differences within the handicapped group as well as between the sample groups in the level of their income.[39] Thus, just over one-quarter of handicapped young people with very stable employment records had net incomes of less than £20 per week (none under £10), but 63 per cent of those with very *un*stable records had low incomes (15 per cent under £10). Those currently without work, and therefore receiving state benefits such as supplementary benefit were concentrated in this unstable, low income group. This trend was confirmed by the experience of other sample groups. Four-fifths of the special help group and seven-tenths of the would benefit group with very stable employment records had weekly incomes of over £20; while two-thirds and two-fifths of the very unstable had incomes of less than £20. The vast majority (86 per cent) of the non-handicapped with very stable histories had incomes of £20 or more.

Subemployment and stability

The fact that many of the handicapped young people had very low incomes was obviously related to the type of work they did as well as to their greater experience of underemployment. The concept of *sub-employment* has been introduced in the American literature to reflect the recognition by some researchers and policy-makers in that country, that unemployment is only one factor in a large number of interrelated symptoms of labour market disadvantage. 'Problems like low wages, job instability, menial work, low skills, poor worker-motivation, discrimination, poor job information, and inadequate job-access seemed equally to demand attention'.[40] Thus the concept of subemployment encompassed not only the unemployed, but also those working part-time who wanted full-time work, low wage earners and those missing from official counts of unemployment. According to Gordon the concept represented the merging of separate concerns for poverty and underemployment based on the recognition that jobs with low wages were central not only to the problem of poverty but also to underemployment.[41]

Although we did not have the data to operationalise the concept of subemployment, it was important to this account because it represented the starting point for a challenge to assumptions surrounding job stability. Sociological research, notably by Liebow, suggested in the late 1960s that instability in work histories provided a key distinction between the poor and the non-poor.[42] Others attributed the causes of this instability largely to individual pathology.[43] At the same time a growing body of literature was pointing to the link between fluctuating demand and instability and the need to study labour market as well as individual factors.[44]

This research on 18-year-olds has shown that many young people were working in poor conditions, were dissatisfied with their jobs and felt insecure (see Chapter 5). Many of them got jobs that lacked training. Thus the previous shorthand expressions 'very stable' and 'very unstable' must not be taken to imply labelling of a set of personal characteristics. Evidence from this survey suggests that certain *jobs,* particularly in the semi-skilled and unskilled groups, may have de-stabilising influences. In effect, some jobs seemed to encourage instability. Ideally these should be distinguished from those jobs that are unstable because they are short-term or seasonal.

The crucial question that remains, however, is why some young people seem to react to the de-stabilising characteristics of jobs more readily than others. In this survey more of the handicapped than non-handicapped changed jobs, but there were wide differences in the types of work they did. Amongst the handicapped, however, 8 per cent of the physically handicapped had held four jobs or more compared with 24 per cent of the ESN(M) and 33 per cent of the maladjusted young people.[45] Although there were differences between these groups in the type of work they did it would appear that individual characteristics and employers perceptions of them interact with job characteristics and result in relative stability or instability.

This focus on job stability or instability suggests that conventional wisdom on young job-changers may in fact underestimate the strength of factors in different jobs which encourage instability: poor conditions, lack of social contact, lack of responsibility, menial work, and so on. A body of young people may in fact be successfully *resisting* job-changing (especially in a period of high unemployment, when to change jobs may result in indefinite unemployment). Thus many of those young people with stable employment histories in our sample may simply have been 'better at', or more resigned to,[46] resisting adverse work conditions. Others of course had escaped some of the worst aspects of predominantly manual employment by gaining jobs of higher status.

In addition to certain de-stabilising effects of particularly low skilled employment, there are some jobs which are by definition, unstable or insecure. As well as temporary and seasonal work there is a category of jobs which are 'age restrictive', which require young people for short periods. In his study of ESN boys in Edinburgh, Jackson found that 21 per cent of all jobs were drawn from one category – sales workers and roundsmen – and that the initial employment was expected not to last longer than one year.[47] (See also the case-study of Sharon in Chapter 3.) Studies such as Jackson's and our own indicate the need for further research on the structure and conditions of different jobs and the underlying reasons for instability.

Some early theories of labour market entry stressed adjustment, 'feet-finding' and trying different jobs to find satisfaction.[48] But this research indicates that for many young workers the search for such rewards is fruitless and that job-changing may be more a function of the individual's reaction to the objective conditions of the working environment. These findings support Carter's conclusion that:

'Most job-changes do *not* represent "a personal struggle" to find an occupation in which "needs for expression, for security and for recognition" will be met; they are to be understood, merely, as a coming to terms with the world of work which is largely bereft of such positive satisfactions'.[49] This process proved most difficult for handicapped young people because they were most likely to be doing unskilled jobs and because they were least likely to adjust quickly to the demands of such work. For many of them the cost of instability proved to be underemployment.

Summary

Handicapped young people had less stable employment records than other groups. The non-handicapped were twice as likely as the handicapped to be very stable. The handicapped were more than twice as likely to have very unstable employment records. Physically handicapped young people had the most stable histories and were the best in adjusting to their jobs. Those handicapped young people in farming and agricultural work, engineering and service jobs were more stable than unstable. It was in the building and industrial manual sectors that those with unstable employment records were concentrated. Handicapped young people with very stable employment histories were four times more likely than the unstable to be in the skilled non-manual class and half as likely to be unskilled. The importance of a successful transition from school to work was again demonstrated. Those with very unstable employment histories were five times more likely than the very stable to have two or more minor nervous complaints. Those with very stable employment records were less likely than the very unstable to have received special help for behaviour difficulties.

10

Employers and Handicapped Young People

The previous analysis of job stability and underemployment has indicated a need for further research on the structure of different jobs and handicapped and other young people's reactions to the various objective conditions of work. Explanations of the problems of school-leavers and of those of the handicapped in particular, have tended to be couched in individualistic terms, rather than showing them as the results of a particular social opportunity structure and its interaction with changing economic factors. The handicapped young person may be well- or less well-prepared for a working life, whilst still at school, and careers advice may be detailed or non-existent. But ultimately his or her chances of obtaining a job depend on acceptance by an employer. Employers' attitudes towards, and perceptions of, the handicapped thus play an important part in determining the ability of the young people to get and keep work and the kinds of employment they can enter. Yet few studies in this country have investigated the attitudes and perceptions of employers in relation to the handicapped.

An employer's knowledge of handicap may be limited or, possibly, detailed only in a few areas of impairment or disability. Their expectations of the abilities of handicapped people in such cases will be distorted, and they may underestimate the handicapped persons' potential, whilst not fully recognising all their needs. This chapter examines the results of a brief questionnaire sent to the employers of the young people in the study. First I explore the link between employers' requirements for a set of personal characteristics in employees and the social division of employment opportunities.

Employment recruitment and discrimination

The importance of employers in determining an individual's experience of work has not been reflected (in this country at least) by detailed research into their perceptions of the employability of different social groups, such as handicapped young people. Previous research has shown that handicapped young people are most likely *not* to possess the personal qualities that employers look for. A study of 116 employers (mostly large firms) by a National Youth Employment Council (NYEC) Working Party in 1972, found that 'most employers emphasised that personality, alertness, and other *personal* qualities were more important to them than "paper qualifications"'.[1] This was particularly true for employers seeking operatives or apprentices.

The Working Party's survey of careers officers indicated that 57 per cent of vacancies for boys and 65 per cent of vacancies for girls at *below* craft level, specified 'smart appearance' or 'mental alertness' or both.[2] Some firms were using selection tests for recruitment at this low level. About two-fifths of the young people in the NYEC survey were described by careers officers as having 'smart appearance' or being 'mentally alert'.[3] Underemployed handicapped young people in this study had most often been classified at school as ESN or maladjusted and came from social backgrounds which may loosely be termed as deprived – their fathers were most likely to be in manual, low-skill employment or to be unemployed, and they had often lived in council housing. Their disadvantage in the labour market bore out the findings of the NYEC survey, which showed that handicapped, ESN and illiterate young people were least likely to enter employment and that those with a 'smart appearance' or who were 'mentally alert' were most likely to obtain jobs.[4]

Employers' expectations of young people and of the educational system have been expressed by the Confederation of British Industry (CBI):

> 'Put in its simplest terms, employers are looking for competence in the basic skills of literacy and numeracy and in general communication skills, which are seen to be the basic abilities essential for anyone in adult life, whether as a private citizen or in any sphere of employment. With these abilities, they would couple qualities of reasoning, independence and adaptability, as well as purpose and motivation, which are essential for survival in an increasingly demanding and competitive world of work.'[5]

In echoing the views of employers and employers' federations[6] the CBI were effectively marking the limits of the work achievements and labour market success of handicapped young people. It is comforting to note that some employers, for example Swan Hunter and Vickers on Tyneside, have introduced remedial teaching in mathematics and literacy into their training schemes.[7]

There are of course other factors which may present barriers to employment for handicapped young people – their capacity for employment at different skill levels, the requirements for different types of jobs, the level of technology and overall demand are some – but the employers' decisions on recruitment and the strength of their demand for certain attributes are clearly of crucial importance. Two main kinds of attributes have become relevant to employment along with the division of labour in western industrial societies: ascriptive characteristics, including sex, race, social class and age; and personal characteristics, including attitudes, skills, personality and credentials.[8] It is the latter, with some ascriptive factors, that have become significant, in determining access to employment at different levels. As Bowles and Gintis argue: 'Even the relationship between social class background and economic success operate in large measure through differences in personal characteristics associated with differential family status. Employers never ask about social background'.[9]

Employers in the private sector have as their primary goals maximum output and profit. One result of the dominance of these pursuits seems to be the growth and perpetuation of stereotyped ideas of 'unproductive' workers. In view of the poor record of nationalised industries in complying with quota regulations under the 1944 Employment (Disabled Persons) Act (by which all employers of more than 20 people are required to employ registered disabled people as 3 per cent of their workforce) there is little indication that state intervention encourages a departure from the private sector model. Two interrelated social phenomena may be distinguished in the creation and persistence of such stereotyped ideas and so contribute to an explanation of what is effectively discrimination against handicapped young people by some sections of the employment system. These phenomena are the social division of life chances, which has been discussed previously, and the social construction of beliefs.

Employers' attitudes to the handicapped

There is evidence, predominantly from the United States, that employers regard individuals with impairments as undesirable employees.[10] Different types of impairment evoke different responses from employers[11] and ex-mental patients are often among those least likely to be hired.[12] At the same time it has been shown that employers underestimate the work capacity of disabled people[13] including ex-mental patients.[14] The problem of employers saying one thing and doing another is raised below, but the most important question is why many employers seem to act in a largely negative way towards disabled and handicapped persons? And furthermore, why do their stereotyped ideas persist despite their experience of employing such people?

An explanation of the continuance of stereotyped ideas was provided by the work of Behrand on financial incentives. In an investigation of firms which adopted payment-by-results methods she noted that there was no valid statistical proof that such methods resulted in higher labour effort.[15] Yet most of the managerial staff *believed* that payment-by-results increased labour production. This raises the crucial distinction between faith or belief and fact: 'the results *expected* from payment-by-results have acquired the status of *achieved* results in spite of the lack of factual proof of their achievement'.[16] The use of financial incentive schemes became associated with generalised beliefs about worker-motivation. Furthermore, when exposed to the actual working of the payment systems, beliefs became modified, but only in relation to individual workers. The general belief associated with a fictional 'average worker' persisted.

The relevance of these findings to our discussion of employment opportunities for handicapped people is obvious. A system of beliefs based partly on the logic of stratification and partly on experience: that those with the least qualifications or with adverse personal characteristics are necessarily poor or unstable workers may be reinforced by the similarly negative attitude of some other employers. (Perhaps the failure of government to enforce the quota scheme further reinforces this belief). There is, in fact, no sustained challenge to the belief. If a handicapped person is hired and not given even minimal support or training and subsequently leaves, this may add further support to the belief; if the handicapped worker stays and is productive he or she may be classed as a special case.[17]

Survey of employers

A short questionnaire was designed for use with employers in order
to discover how they perceived handicapped people in relation to
the jobs done in their particular company, firm or shop. Employers
were asked whether they employed any young handicapped people
and what special treatment, if any, these young people received.
The questionnaire was sent by post to 156 employers throughout
Britain. They were selected from the employers of the young people
in the sample, each having recently employed one of the 18-year-
olds (not necessarily handicapped). Their addresses were selected
to achieve a representative regional spread, so that the employment
problems peculiar to any one area would not unduly bias the replies.
Usually the questionnaire was addressed to the manager of the company, except for large organisations, where it was sent to the
personnel or recruitment officer. The accompanying letter request-
ed that the views of 'the person directly responsible for recruiting
young people' should be given in the questionnaire. Also it
explained the nature and purpose of the study which had already
collected the views of young people, parents and teachers, and
stressed the need for 'a balanced picture' which could be better
achieved if employers' views were taken into account.

Although each employer was told on what basis his organisation
had been selected, at no point was the name of the young person
who was (or had been) working for him revealed, nor whether or
not this person was handicapped. Three months after the questionnaire was first sent out in February/March 1977, another letter with
a copy of the questionnaire was sent to all non-responders. Five
letters were returned, from companies who were no longer trading,
so that the final sample size was 151. Sixty-seven replies were
eventually received – a response rate of 44 per cent.

Stereotyped ideas of the handicapped

Employers were asked to describe the type of people they *immediately* imagined handicapped school-leavers to be. From the sixty-
seven employers there were eight who did not reply to this question,
saying that they had no stereotyped ideas. From the rest of the
replies, however, it was clear that many people reacted with images
of observable, physical impairments. Thus, 44 per cent of the
employers wrote only of physical or sensory handicaps, and most of

these simply named a few specific handicapping conditions, for example: 'physically deficient in arms, legs or body'; 'deaf or malformed at birth or handicapped through disease'; 'limbs missing, blind or spastic'; 'partially deaf, poor sight, thalidomide or paralysed limbs'.

Another 32 per cent of employers mentioned both mental and physical handicaps. Usually they did not give a specific type of handicap – the answers consisted of broad categories such as 'physically and mentally handicapped'. Only 15 per cent of employers said that they immediately thought of the 'mentally retarded' or 'backward' young people, although there were two employers who qualified this: 'Children who cannot read or write, or with low IQ'; 'Those with an immature personality (and often low IQ) who would soon be at sea in a large organisation if not supervised and taught, for example, those from a special school'. This last quotation, which revealed some insight into the problems of the educationally subnormal, came from a company which appeared to be sympathetic to the problems of handicapped young people. (Since this company will be mentioned again it will for ease of recognition be called 'company B').

The remaining answers to this question revealed narrow or vague concepts, not linked to any specific handicap. For example, 'those registered by the department of employment', or those with 'a superficial disability', or 'largely unsuitable for this type of industry because of the wet, slippery floors and damp conditions and production line processes'. The question was aimed at obtaining immediate reactions to the idea of handicap in young people and not a carefully considered and comprehensive reply. So it is perhaps not surprising that many of the answers were expressed in such narrow terms. But it is clear that physical handicaps, and particularly those affecting limbs, hearing or sight, were the ones which came immediately to mind. Educational subnormality, although more common in occurence, was not so readily recognised as a handicap.

Other handicaps which received no mention at all, were the less easily observable 'physical' handicaps, such as heart disorders, epilepsy and asthma. Persons with these conditions do not *look* handicapped in the way that a wheelchair-bound, blind, or deaf person so obviously does. Maladjustment, as shown through disturbed behaviour patterns, was also not included in the stereotypes of handicap. However in answers to a later question on the preparation of non-handicapped young people for work, a number of employers complained about the lack of basic literacy skills and of indiscipline amongst young people. It is possible that these complaints were reinforced by experiences with educationally subnormal or maladjusted young employees. These two groups of handicapped young people were liable to underemployment and unstable work histories.

In part this poor experience is a reflection of the fact that in all bureaucratic organisations authority and order are key factors. These young people are apparently least likely to behave and obey rules, or to possess the personal qualities of obedience and deference. If employers on the other hand fail to recognise any indiscipline as a manifestation of some underlying difficulty, the young person will be sacked and the employer's stereotype of the unstable worker reinforced. In addition this stereotype will also be encouraged by the acceptance of high wastage as normal by some employers. This is particularly true in the distributive sector.[18]

Employment of handicapped young people

Firms were asked whether they employed any handicapped young people under the age of 25 years. Half of the employers – 34 companies – said that they did. It came as no surprise that the larger the organisation, the more likely it was to employ handicapped young people – statistically it is to be expected that an organisation of several thousand employees is more likely to have at least one handicapped young person than a firm with fewer than 20 employees. The very small organisations (fewer than 20 employees) did not employ any recognisably handicapped young people, and in fact six of the seven such employers, in answer to a later question, said that young people were not an essential part of their labour force in any case. In contrast to this the organisations with 20–100 employees were most likely to have had more than 1 per cent handicapped young people, and this was particularly true when the company was not part of a group of companies nor a national organisation. Overall the companies with predominantly manual occupations were more likely than those with predominantly non-manual occupations, to employ handicapped young people: 60 per cent of the former compared to 37 per cent of the latter did so.

These results show the number of employers who *knowingly* employed handicapped young people. It is likely that others employed young people, unaware that they were handicapped, or without classifying them as 'handicapped'. For example, one employer who claimed that he employed no handicapped young people revealed in answer to a later question: 'we also engage educationally subnormal girls to work in our bindery department'. This emphasised the fact that ESN young people were not part of the general stereotype of handicap.

The types of handicap present in the sample of young employees were less biased towards physical handicap than the answers to the questions reported above might suggest (see Chapter 2). However in later questions employers were given examples of the types of handicap which they might have encountered and these included mental handicap and educational handicap. Given this as guidance, 29 per cent of employers said they employed both physically and mentally handicapped young people, 22 per cent had young employees who suffered from physical handicaps only and 18 per cent employed mentally, but not physically, handicapped young people. Some of the employers in the largest organisations gave extensive lists of handicaps not mentioned by others. For example, in one company with almost 5000 employees there were young people with the following handicaps: 'Two with paralysis, two blind in one eye, two who had lost a limb, one with arthritis, one with Cronin's disease, one with a hearing defect, one diabetic'. It was surprising that such a large company apparently had no recorded instances of ESN(M) young people. Another employer listed a wide variety of handicaps, many of which were not mentioned by other employers: 'Colour blindness, vertigo, claustrophobia, asthma, partial deafness, personality disorder, diabetes, cardiac condition, epilepsy, paralysis'. Obviously the first three conditions listed here are only 'handicaps' in certain types of work situation, and would not be considered as handicaps by many employers for their types of jobs. Again it is interesting to find that in this large organisaion, of 8000 employees, there were apparently no ESN(M) young people.

Finally company B employed 'Spastics, those with a low IQ, one blind person, several deaf and dumb, one with very poor sight, one polio victim, four with Down's syndrome and several epileptics'. In addition, this employer said he would consider employing people with 'psychiatric disorders, for example schizoid; muscular dystrophy, hydrocephalus'. The range of handicaps listed here, covering physical, sensory, mental and emotional handicaps, was broader than that encountered in most other organisations and again illustrated this particular company's insight into the nature of handicap. This broad-minded approach was also reflected in company B's answer to the question about the types of work that handicapped young people did in the firm. 'Any, depending on the residual abilities.' This emphasis on ability, rather than disability and incapacity, was not encountered in such a clearly defined form in most of the other firms.

Training and the handicapped

All employers claimed that the handicapped young people were very well or fairly well accepted by workmates. Almost half of the companies with handicapped young people employed them only in unskilled jobs, as labourers, cleaners or porters for example. As a result of this, comparatively few handicapped young people received any training other than on-the-job training to learn their task. In fact there were only two instances in which employers specifically said that handicapped young people took apprenticeships, and even then the proportions of the handicapped taking such training were low. For example, in one large company, employing forty physically handicapped young people, 95 per cent of all young people were apprentices, but amongst the handicapped this applied to only 3 per cent.

In another large company, where 80 per cent of young people were apprentices, only two of the ten handicapped young people were serving apprenticeships: 'This is solely because most of our disabled youngsters are mentally disabled'. The assumption that retarded or educationally subnormal young people were not able to benefit from apprenticeships was also suggested by other employers. For example, the largest organisation in the survey included fifteen handicapped young people in its staff of 13 000 – five were paraplegics who held professional jobs, whilst one other paraplegic and nine educationally subnormal young people held unskilled manual jobs. Whilst the majority of young people in this organisation served apprenticeships none of the fifteen handicapped young people did so, although five or six of them had been on courses arranged by the firm.

Very few employers gave any special consideration to the employment or training of their handicapped young employees. Three employers said that they would allow extra time for such a person to 'settle in', and in another instance management was prepared to pay 'special attention' to the handicapped. In two cases, it was said that existing training would be modified to help the handicapped. In only three other companies were any special measures taken. Company B provided 'special car parks' and 'help with mobility on site, for example, a helper to push wheel chairs'. Two other companies had adapted furniture or equipment, and one company took care that wheelchair-bound people worked on the ground floor. These three companies were all large, having 750, 4 800 and 7 300 employees. There was no evidence of any smaller companies adapting furniture or equipment.

Recruitment

There were three main avenues by which the young handicapped people obtained their jobs, according to their employers: through a careers officer; in answer to advertisements, and by personal contact – either by the school, or through parents or friends already working for the firm. However, whilst careers officers were mentioned by companies of all sizes, advertisements were more likely to be the method by which the largest firms (those with more than 500 employees) recruited the handicapped. Personal contact was often the means of recruitment amongst smaller firms (100–500 employees). However, these differences were slight. According to employers. Jobcentres played relatively little part as a means of obtaining work for handicapped young people.

Firms not employing handicapped young people

What of the firms who did not employ any handicapped young people? They were asked if they would employ such a person; what handicaps they would be prepared to accept, or why they would not employ handicapped people. Eighteen employers (out of thirty-three not already employing the handicapped) said that they would consider employing a handicapped young person, but eight of these were only willing to take on the physically handicapped. Three others specified requirements which might rule out many handicapped people. Examples of employers' replies are as follows: one employer would only consider employing 'a blind telephonist';

another would take on 'the partially sighted for turning, or the partly disabled for manual bench work'; another 'those crippled but able to use a hand-operated machine'. An employer who already employed one deaf person would consider 'deaf people, people with a finger amputation and epileptics'. The owner of a family business, who employed a deaf and dumb person, commented that he could 'easily employ other deaf and dumb people but had never been approached'. One manager who was willing to take on handicapped people added that there were 'no adequate toilets for paraplegics'; but another was willing to use 'simple special facilities' to help a physically handicapped person. Another requirement mentioned by one employer, was 'a "normal" appearance'.

Many of those not employing handicapped young people appeared to answer this question with specific jobs and specific handicaps in mind, and few took the apparently open-minded approach of one employer, who would employ 'anyone who could fill the vacancy, regardless of handicap'. However, previous research indicates that even where employers say they are willing to take on handicapped young people, in practice they are less likely to.[19]

Amongst the eleven employers who said that they would not consider employing handicapped young people, it was clear that many were referring mainly to physical handicap and barriers to mobility. For example, one employer explained: 'our factory personnel are engaged in handling rolls of heavy material – mainly standing, operating machines. Our offices are on top of a three-storey building with no lifts'. Safety aspects were also emphasised by several employers: 'All our process areas have wet floors and we have a lot of dangerous equipment, filling-machines, conveyors, fork-lift trucks. Our own staff have a fair number of accidents because of these conditions, and it would be unfair to expose handicapped people to these processes'. The owner of a small filling station felt he could not employ handicapped young people because of, 'The difficulty of operating pumps on a busy forecourt'. In fact he had for some time employed a 'one-armed educationally subnormal youth for the sake of keeping him occupied. Now, a more suitable job has been found for him'.

Specific handicapping conditions

All the employers were asked what percentage of jobs at their plant could be carried out by young people with various types of handicap. Answers to these questions bore out the statement by the CBI above and the actual experiences of handicapped young people in the study. About one-fifth of the employers did not answer this question. Some of them commented: 'Each case is considered on its merits in relation to a particular job'. Ten different types of handicapping conditions were listed and for the most part about half the companies felt that no jobs could be carried out by people with any such conditions.

No employer felt that any of the jobs in his company could be done by 'a person confined to a wheelchair who cannot manage controlled arm-movements, but who was intelligent'. It was, perhaps, surprising that they did not visualise as suitable any non-manual jobs, with special aids. 'A wheelchair-bound person with unrestricted upper body movements' could apparently have coped with some jobs in about half the firms, but only one employer felt that more than 30 per cent of jobs would have been suitable. The example given of 'an epileptic person, but one not likely to have a fit' provoked some extreme reactions. One half of the companies with predominantly non-manual workers, but only one third of companies employing predominantly manual workers, felt that *no* jobs were suitable. Yet one-third of the predominantly 'manual' firms, and less than a quarter of 'non-manual' firms felt that more than half the jobs could be done by such an epileptic person. In fact there were six companies who felt that *all* their jobs could be undertaken by a person with this handicap.

Another example of 'A person unable to read or write well, slow in thinking, but physically fit' was felt by about one-third of employers, in predominantly 'manual' companies, to be unsuitable for any jobs; the proportion in 'non-manual' companies was one-half. 'A mentally handicapped young person who can carry out simple tasks with supervision' was felt to be entirely unsuitable by four out of five of all employers, and in only four cases was it felt that more than 5 per cent of jobs would be possible. 'Emotionally unstable young people, liable to bursts of temper' were similarly rejected, and in only one-fifth of non-manual companies, and one-sixth of manual companies, were any jobs felt to be suitable. Company B's answer, however, was that such employees would 'soon stop losing their temper'.

The most 'acceptable' handicap amongst firms with mainly manual work, was deafness (or partial deafness) and more than one in five such firms felt that 50 per cent or more of their jobs were suitable for the deaf. One-half of 'non-manual' firms, but less than one-third of 'manual' firms, felt that *no* jobs were suitable for the deaf. In the case of 'young people with chest complaints' these proportions were reversed and two-thirds of the 'non-manual' firms felt that at least some jobs could be undertaken by such a person. Very few jobs were felt to be suitable for the blind and partially sighted – two-thirds of the employers said that no jobs were suitable. 'Young people with back complaints' surprisingly appeared to be more acceptable in companies with predominantly manual jobs, and as many as one-sixth felt that more than a half of the jobs were suitable.

Overall, then, deafness and educational subnormality were rated by employers as most acceptable handicaps, whilst physical immobility (even without accompanying intellectual impairment) and emotional instability were least acceptable.

Improving employment opportunities

Employers were asked whether they would be more inclined to employ handicapped young people if certain types of help such as guidance about the needs of those with specific handicaps, assistance with training and financial help with training, were available. More than half of the sixty-seven companies would not have welcomed any such help. Amongst the remainder one-quarter cited financial help for training. Guidance in training the handicapped, or, less often, guidance as to the needs of the handicapped, would also have been welcomed in a number of cases. The smallest organisations (those with fewer than 20 employees) were least likely to want these forms of help, and were also the least likely to employ handicapped young people. Furthermore, half the companies who said they would be more inclined to take on handicapped young people if given such help, were already employing such young people.

The questionnaire posed the problem of improving employment opportunities for handicapped shcool leavers. This produced a wide variety of suggestions from employers, although as many as 38 per cent did not feel able to comment. A lack of knowledge as to what the handicapped can achieve, if given adequate support, was evident in some replies. 'Employers need more information about the abilities and disabilities'; 'There should be better statement of their potential – they need selling to industry'; 'There needs to be a greater realisation among employers of the qualities offered by these young people'; 'Many employers do not realise that handicapped young people can be trained to do a job, within their capabilities, as well as, if not better than, able-bodied young people'; 'You need to demonstrate to employers and employees that a handicap does not mean poor productivity nor the need for extra expenditure on supervision.'

Five employers suggested improvements in training schemes; for example, 'Increasing the scope or fields of training to cover as wide an area as possible', or 'Training for specific occupations in their last year at school. Cut deadwood lessons and guide them towards occupational therapy'. Yet other employers would have welcomed assistance, sometimes financial, with training or with other aspects of employing handicapped young people: 'We need other Industrial Training Boards and government assistance with training and adaptation of the work place. To illustrate this I would point out that we would hesitate to employ a paraplegic as we do not have adequate toilet facilities for someone so handicapped'. One answer encompassed a number of points of view: 'So much depends on the type of handicap, attitudes of parents and attitudes of employers towards providing special facilities, especially having regard to the Health and Safety at Work Act. However, joint funding schemes, removing obligations on the employer to finance training, would help. Also there should be specialist liaison between agencies, careers service, educationalists, trade unions and employers on the problems involved'.

The need for closer contact between employers and other agencies was echoed by other answers, many employers complaining that they did not hear about handicapped people seeking work. Some called for 'a personal approach to local employers from the teacher responsible'; 'heads of school and teachers making more contact with individuals in firms'; 'close contact between headmasters and teachers who know a child's ability and companies who may have suitable jobs available'.

Other employers did not see placement activities as the schools' responsibility but suggested better communication with the Employment Services Agency. 'By issuing companies with details of people available for employment and by regular consultation with companies in the possible employment of the people'; or 'a local register held by Jobcentres, with employers receiving advice of possible applicants when a vacancy arises'. Two-way communication was clearly felt to be desirable: 'We advise the Department of Employment of all our vacancies but we rarely hear of handicapped people needing employment'. Closer contact with the handicapped themselves was suggested in one case: 'Handicapped people should be encouraged to go and see employers who advertise normal jobs in the press or through employment agencies'. There did not seem to be any suggestion that employers themselves should act to bring about closer contact.

An enforcement of the quota system was suggested by one employer, whilst another saw an answer in 'reserving a percentage of local government jobs for them' and yet another in 'creating jobs in suitable companies'. This was often the impression given by employers: they were happy for the handicapped to be employed – but in other companies. There were still others who suggested more segregation: 'Regional state workrooms tailored to meet the needs of the handicapped'; 'An increased subsidy and provision of Government-run establishments such as Remploy.' One employer, who incidentally felt that handicapped people would be 'unable to perform the duties' required in any of the jobs in his firm, felt that they would be 'happier segregated'. His suggestion was: 'Set up small establishments where they can perform tasks without feeling out of place, but can feel they are contributing their efforts to worth-while products.'

In conclusion, it can be said that employers seemed to suffer from a lack of communication on all fronts – many had little idea of the potential of handicapped young people, were not informed of such people seeking jobs and were unaware of schemes to aid them in employing and training the handicapped. Furthermore many did not appear to accept that they should, or could, make any effort to employ the handicapped. What is required is, in the words of only one manager, 'A more sympathetic approach by employers.'

Employers and young people

What qualities did employers seek in recruiting young people? In the questionnaire ten qualities were listed and employers were asked to select the three most important. Six employers did not answer this question, and six others gave two selections based on the different types of occupations found within their organisation. So, the following analysis is based on 67 selections. By far the most frequently mentioned quality was general intelligence; this was selected in 82 per cent of answers. Over half the employers chose 'practical ability', whilst 'appearance' was considered important by 42 per cent of the employers. Over one-third also required physical fitness, some of them specifically referring to 'good medical records' or 'good health'. The least likely to be selected were 'verbal ability' and 'ambition' – both chosen only six times each. Academic ability was comparatively low in importance, being chosen by 25 per cent of employers – mainly those in firms with predominantly non-manual jobs, as was the case with verbal ability.

Of course, these findings on the situation facing school-leavers also had some bearing on the plight of the young handicapped. For example, the employers emphasised the importance for young people of training in skills, yet the next chapter shows clearly that the handicapped received little in the way of training (especially in the way of apprenticeships) suggesting that employers did not see them as a source of skill. Nor are employers likely to value the handicapped as a source of 'strength, nimbleness and adaptability', since many employers visualise handicap in terms of physical incapacity.

In view of the importance to employers of 'general intelligence', irrespective of the requirements of the job itself, the ESN(M) school-leaver is at an obvious disadvantage, in competition with his more able peers. Also, because of the socially disadvantaged background which often accompanies educational subnormality, he may well fail to make the grade in terms of his 'appearance' also. For those seeking non-manual jobs an apparent lack of academic ability may be a stumbling block – the physically handicapped may have missed prolonged periods of schooling because of ill-health, and in addition, if attending small special schools, may not have been given the opportunity to take examinations, which might otherwise have provided employers with proof of their academic abilities.

Summary

Previous accounts of the employment problems of handicapped young people were often given purely from the handicapped person's viewpoint. An attempt was made in this study to contact *employers* and determine their perceptions of handicap and their attitudes towards the employment of handicapped young people. Further research in this area is clearly needed.

Employers stress personal attributes such as appearance, general intelligence or mental alertness, even when recruiting for the semi-skilled and unskilled levels. These expectations effectively discriminate against handicapped young people. Part of the basis for the legitimation of this discrimination is to be found in the stratification of life chances and the social construction of beliefs about abilities and motivation. Employers were more likely than not to perceive handicap as physical impairment. Most of them did not recognise ESN(M) or maladjusted young people as handicapped. Only one-half of the employers said that they employed handicapped young people. Very little training was given to the handicapped as compared to that given to the non-handicapped. Deafness and educational subnormality were regarded as being the most acceptable handicaps, whilst physical immobility and emotional instability were the least acceptable.

11

Further Education and Training

The majority of the handicapped school-leavers were of below-average ability in reading, English and mathematics and had taken no formal examinations. They were predominantly in the unskilled and semi-skilled occupational groups. In a society where material rewards and status are attendant in large part on educational success, many young people are by virtue of their lack of educational achievement, doomed to experience underemployment coupled, perhaps at best, with unrewarding work. The fact that unequal educational opportunity is determined to a great extent by social class background implies that radical changes in social structure are necessary to ensure greater equality in education and working life.[1] Postponing consideration of that proposition until the concluding chapter, it may well be assumed that the provision of further education and training facilities operates to counteract the unequal division of educational achievement in schools and so contributes to social mobility. In this chapter we examine the distribution of further education and training opportunities among the 18-year-olds.

Education and the handicapped

There is, of course, no logical reason, at least in social or educational terms, why formal education should cease at a particular age, 16, 18, 40, or any other. Yet this for most people is precisely the effect that a fixed minimum school-leaving age has on their formal educational experiences. This tendency is reinforced by the dominant concern of the educational system for the minority who progress through all of its different stages. Thus there is an enduring paradox in the educational provision of most industrial societies: those who need most education get least. This inequality between the most able and the least able is likely to remain in Britain in the foreseeable future[2] and if evidence from the United States is a good guide, it is likely to become increasingly exaggerated.[3]

The vast majority of handicapped young people leave school at the minimum age, some because they have to. It is *expected* that they will leave at 16 years of age. Obviously if a young person is educationally handicapped, the effects of the handicap are not going to be changed by the simple expedient of leaving school. If the social situation of the handicapped school-leaver – the disadvantage documented earlier – is to be changed, the young person should perhaps be a continuing responsibility, but whose? The need for continued education is seldom recognised by the young person; many are glad to escape from the failure associated with school and are naturally reluctant to undergo 'more of the same'.[4] At the same time, as the previous chapter demonstrated, their need was often not recognised by employers either. This was particularly true for employers of predominantly manual labour.[5]

The vast majority of the handicapped school-leavers in the sample survey reported here, the ESN(M), will never take part in higher education. Previous research has shown that they are also the least likely to be involved in other forms of further education or training.[6] Yet according to the Inner London Education Authority (ILEA), many of the ESN(M) have a higher potential than their achievements would suggest. Through the provision of linked courses while they are still at school, it is being acknowledged more and more, 'that these students can integrate quite effectively into the normal college curriculum'.[7] The rest of this chapter describes how those in the sample took up education and training.

Further education and training courses

There were a number of problems attached to the collection of data about further education and training. The numbers of handicapped young people who had participated in further education in a two-year period after leaving school was likely to be very small. The distinction between further education and training was often difficult to draw consistently. Historically, a distinction between training and further education has been reflected in different institutional settings and responsibilities for meeting the cost. The Training

Services Agency (TSA – now part of the Training Services Division) defined the 'single process' of vocationally orientated learning' in two parts: *training* being concerned with learning job skills (how to do things) and vocationally orientated *further education* as being more concerned with the general concepts involved (why things are done). They also distinguished between vocationally orientated further education and further education which is 'primarily an extension of general education'.[8]

In this project detailed questions were asked about further education and training and at the coding stage the two were separated, primarily on the basis of academic content and sponsoring organisation. Training was defined as specific job training or vocational training, but might have included day-release and other further education courses taken as part of a training course, and this therefore followed the TSA definition. A check was also kept to ensure that answers to the section of the questionnaire on further education and training were consistent with answers to later questions about training related to specific employment.

Further education

According to the Committee of Inquiry into Adult Education (Russell Committee) which reported in 1973: 'there exists an enormous reservoir of human and material resources' which could be released through adult education.[9] This is perhaps most true for the large group of unqualified, educationally disadvantaged young people who leave special schools or units attached to ordinary schools at the minimum school-leaving age.

Only 9 per cent of handicapped young people had taken part in some form of further education since leaving school, 6 per cent were currently doing a course when interviewed. Over half of those participating in further education, were in fact doing an adult literacy course. By contrast 21 per cent of non-handicapped young people had done or were planning to do a course of further education, 29 per cent were still at school or in further education (four-fifths of these intended to go on to higher education).[10]

What kinds of further education had the handicapped young people pursued? Thirteen (including all ten of the ESN(M) who had done some further education) had taken adult literacy courses. Two of the physically handicapped were at technical colleges doing secretarial courses and office studies; another was at the National Star Centre for Disabled Youth doing woodwork, English and reading. A 'delicate' young man was also at the centre taking 'O' levels. Another 'delicate' person was in a sixth-form college doing 'A' levels. Partially sighted young people were taking courses in horticulture and accounting. A deaf young man was at a college of further education taking a City and Guilds catering course, while one ESN(M) and one with partial-hearing were respectively learning to read and studying English. Maladjusted young people had taken courses in business studies (OND), maths, physics and computing, catering and 'O' level subjects.

Training courses

Twenty-one per cent of the handicapped young people (excluding the ESN(S)) had taken part, or were intending to take part, in a training course.[11] Eight per cent were currently on training courses, 10 per cent had finished courses and 3 per cent were planning to go on courses. Here 'training' included apprenticeships with day-release (28 per cent of those who had taken courses); training which entailed attendance at a technical college; secretarial training; attendance at a government training centre, adult training centre or employment rehabilitation centre; training in the armed services and on-the-job training lasting four or more weeks. Thirty-two per cent of the special help group had taken or intended to take a training course; over half of these were apprenticeships. The figures for the would benefit and non-handicapped groups were 27 per cent (over half of which were apprenticeships) and 51 per cent (half of which were apprenticeships).

Over half the handicapped young people in apprenticeships were in the skilled manual class or higher. Of the non-handicapped apprentices 92 per cent were skilled manual or higher, and the vast majority of those doing vocational training were, by definition, in either the professional, intermediate or skilled non-manual social class.[12] The numbers involved were small, but there was some indication that the handicapped young people from ordinary schools were more likely than those from special schools to become apprentices (50 per cent compared to 15 per cent).[13] The largest group of young people from special schools went on to adult training centres (30 per cent) followed by technical colleges (18 per cent).

There were also differences based on father's social class. The handicapped young people in further education whose fathers were in the top three social classes (based on occupational groups) were most likely to be found in technical colleges or in vocational training; while those whose fathers were skilled manual workers were concentrated in apprenticeships.[14] The children of semi-skilled and unskilled workers were more often in technical colleges or adult training centres.

Sources of information and advice about courses

All the young people in the study were asked if they had spoken to anyone about the possibility of taking the further education or training course. For those intending to do further education or training official channels of advice proved to be of greater importance than they were during the search for work. Fourteen per cent of the handicapped and 19 per cent of the non-handicapped had not consulted anyone.[15] Twenty-seven per cent of the handicapped compared with 50 per cent of the non-handicapped had consulted more than one person. Large proportions of both groups, (35 per cent and 49 per cent) had spoken to their parents; and 6 and 13 per cent respectively had consulted friends. One-fifth of the former and just over one-fifth of the latter had spoken to a careers or other teacher. Sixteen per cent of the handicapped and 9 per cent of the non-handicapped had spoken to a careers officer; 6 per cent and 18 per cent respectively had spoken to their employer or training officer at work.

Within the handicapped group there were interesting and statistically very significant differences between ESN(M) and physically handicapped young people. The ESN(M) were less likely to have talked to someone about further education or training, an indication that many (86 per cent) of them did not see these as important or feasible post-school pursuits. The physically handicapped and control group were more likely to have discussed it with someone (43 per cent and 33 per cent)[16] Three-quarters of the maladjusted young people had not spoken to anyone about further education or training.

Work-based training

All the young people who had worked were asked about any training they had received in their current or latest job. Table 11.1 shows that the non-handicapped were much more likely than the handicapped to be formally trained rather than simply shown what to do. Differences between the handicapped and non-handicapped were statistically very significant.

TABLE 11.1   *Training received in last or current job (%)*

Type of training	Sample group			
	Handi-capped	Special help	Would benefit	Non-handi-capped
None	8.6	9.2	(7.7)	6.8
Shown what to do in 1 day or less	35.3	27.8	(20.5)	9.4
Shown in more than 1 day	37.1	35.2	(20.5)	18.9
Training course, one, or more than one week	5.2	7.4	(12.8)	18.9
Apprenticeship – with day-release	3.4	13.0	(15.4)	29.7
Apprenticeship – no release	4.3	5.5	(12.8)	2.7
Other day-release	1.7	0.0	(5.1)	9.4
Evening classes	0.9	1.8	(0.0)	1.3
Promotion course	0.0	0.0	(0.0)	2.7
Don't know	3.4	0.0	(5.1)	0.0
Total	100	100	100	100
Number	116	54	39	74

Handicapped *vs* non-handicapped: $X^2 = 60.2$, 12 degrees of freedom, $p < 0.001$.

In their recent research on school leavers in Scotland Weir and Nolan found that a similarly small proportion of their *non*-handicapped sample had received only minimal training. Only 10 per cent of those 'in training' considered that their only instruction had been 'standing next to Nellie.'[17] Whereas over half of the young people in Maizels's Willesden sample were shown what to do by fellow-workers rather than by specially trained instructors.[18] The National Youth Employment Council survey in 1972, found that a very high proportion of disabled, illiterate and ESN young people lacked educational qualifications and those who were employed had been recruited for jobs which offered little or no training.[19] Various studies have pointed to a decline in the quality of training, particularly of craft-training.[20] But this study has indicated that training for handicapped young people working below craft level was virtually non-existent.

Training and skill-level

The extent and quality of job-training are clearly dependent on type of work and level of skill. Reduced sample numbers prevented a full analysis, but handicapped young people in skilled and unskilled jobs could be contrasted.[21] Nearly 25 per cent of those in skilled manual jobs were shown what to do at work, in *less* than one day, compared with 41 per cent of unskilled workers. Thirty-two per cent of the skilled manual, 33 per cent of the semi-skilled and 48 per cent of the unskilled were shown what to do in their job in *more* than one day. None of the skilled manual, but 10 per cent of the semi-skilled and 9 per cent of the unskilled, received *no* training.

So, the majority of handicapped young people (four-fifths) who did not receive any training were doing semi-skilled or unskilled jobs. Also the majority of those who were simply *shown* what to do, rather than formally trained, were in these lowest classes (four-fifths of those shown what to do in one day or less and two-thirds of those shown in more than one day). Most of the non-handicapped (92 per cent) who were in apprenticeships with day-release were in the skilled manual class or higher. Other studies have confirmed the relationship between skill level and quality of training – the higher the skill the better the training.[22] Research by the Medical Research Council showed that 80 per cent of boys who left school early and entered unskilled employment received no training of any sort.[23]

It is not intended to imply that handicapped young people in semi-skilled and unskilled jobs should receive a similar training to those in, say, skilled manual apprenticeships. But training is an essential feature of manpower policy for the handicapped and other young people for two reasons. It ensures an overall improvement in the skill of the worker and so contributes to his chances of upward skill-mobility and secondly, it contributes to increasing satisfaction with work. The need for job improvement was touched on in Chapter 5. This was reinforced by the discovery of a close relationship between job stability and training and also some association between happiness in work and job training. Those handicapped young people who were very happy or happy in their latest job were more likely than the unhappy to be apprentices or to have been on a formal training course.[24] Eighteen per cent of those who received no training or were simply shown what to do in their job were not very happy or were very unhappy (excluding those *not* currently working). None of those who had been on a formal training course, day release or apprenticeship were unhappy or not very happy.

Demand for further education and training

All the young people who were *not* taking nor intending to take a full-time further education or training course were asked if, given the chance, they would want to take part in further education or training, either on a full-time or part-time basis. Substantial proportions of *all* the sample groups would have liked to do further education or training.[25] Fifty-two per cent of the handicapped young people and 39 per cent of the non-handicapped said that they would have liked to take part in further education or training. Twenty-six per cent of the former and 12 per cent of the latter wanted full-time courses. When this group and those already taking full-time education or training courses in the next year were combined, exactly equal proportions (62 per cent) of handicapped and non-handicapped young people were either already engaged on, or planning, courses of further education or training, or said they wanted to take such courses.

Equal proportions of the two main sample groups wanted to do further education courses.[26] Three per cent of both handicapped and non-handicapped young people wanted full-time further education and 5 per cent part-time. In view of the very poor employment position of the handicapped group, outlined in previous chapters, it was not surprising that a greater proportion of them than of the non-handicapped wanted to be trained for a skill. Eighteen per cent of the handicapped compared with 3 per cent of the non-handicapped wanted full-time training and 10 per cent compared with 17 per cent wanted part-time training. Comparisons within the handicapped group on the basis of social class showed that 40 per cent of those in skilled non-manual or manual work did not want further education or training compared with 43 per cent of the semi-skilled and unskilled but 20 per cent of the former compared with 37 per cent of the latter wanted to be trained for a skill.[27] Eleven per cent of the skilled and 5 per cent of the unskilled wanted vocational training.

A second chance?

These findings did not provide any indication that handicapped young people were, through further education and training facilities, being enabled to overcome their educational handicaps and disadvantage in the labour market. Rather, opportunities to benefit from these provisions were directly related to the level of the job taken when they left school and therefore, unequal access to post-school provision reinforced rather than counteracted educational handicaps. It appeared that handicapped young people were effectively trapped in their disadvantaged situation in the labour market. To gain access to skill-training and further education through day-release they must have first secured employment above the unskilled level. To gain skilled employment they must have demonstrated educational achievement or have projected a personal image which belied their school and home background, without training or encouragement.

Significant proportions of all the sample groups wanted some kind of further education or training. However, regardless of the extent of any *expressed* need for further education or training, there are clearly sound moral, economic and educational reasons for improving the scope and coverage of such facilities. There was a link between training opportunities and job stability and job satisfaction. Employers may be amazed by the high labour turnover in their industry, as for example in the clothing or catering industries, and yet baulk at the cost of job-training and job-improvement. Worse still, some simply accept the high turnover of young people as a fact of life.[28] The social costs of monotonous, boring work may be reduced by job-improvement and training. The economic arguments for improving the skill of the workforce are well known. For example, in its first annual report, the Manpower Services Commission argued that inflationary pressure was coming largely from the bottlenecks and shortages of skilled labour in the areas of expansion. The Training Services Agency (TSA) has estimated that three-fifths of school-leavers receive no formal training at all,[29] and this research has shown that it is the handicapped, particularly the least able intellectually, who are most likely *not* to be trained nor to take part in further education. The main reason for this failure is the attitude of both the employers and the young people.

Employers and training

Responsibility for vocational training currently rests primarily with employers. As with other facilities and benefits (see Chapter 5) the extent of training is principally determined by the type of work done by the young people. Apprenticeships are the traditional route to skilled manual status in British industry. Few of the handicapped were in apprenticeships, and as the TSA point out, the level of day-release for other employees is low. Girls get much less day-release than boys, and day-release is very low in operative-based industries and some services. Employers in these sectors question the necessity for training or for paying for the education of young workers. The Committee appointed by the Minister of Education in November 1962 to investigate ways of increasing day-release, found that employers 'insisted that day-release should be regarded as a privilege'. However, they did admit that the time had now passed when the employer should feel entirely free to grant or withhold it.[30] Employers saw the cost and the resulting disruption of production as major barriers to providing day-release.

In other European countries, training plays a much more significant role in the lives of school-leavers. In France, the length of apprenticeships has been reduced to two years full-time study on an integrated course of education and training. Those young people not in an apprenticeship are guaranteed the right to paid study-leave of 100 hours per year. The West German government has declared its intention to confer education rights on all young people, not only those with proven academic ability. Employers must have training skills and knowledge of teaching methods or they have to appoint a qualified training officer. In Sweden only 10 per cent of school-leavers go straight into jobs and receive no vocational education at all.

Although the majority of handicapped young people not on a further education or training course actually wanted one, a significant minority (two-fifths) did not. Handicapped young people may feel that they are unsuitable for further education or training. Educational 'failures' may not want to repeat some of the trials of learning. Education and training are, perhaps, too closely associated with schooling in the young person's mind. In short, young people are unprepared for further education and training. 'For many boys, school thankfully marks the end of education and it therefore takes them some time to adjust to the necessity of "going back to school", be it college or training centre.'[31] It is especially alarming that such a tiny fraction of the handicapped had done a further education course, since their *need* for continued education was unquestionable. As the Russell Report pointed out, educationally we are still two nations 'and among the educational "have-nots" the needs are vast'.[32]

It is shown in Chapter 13 that handicapped young people were more likely than others to have had to leave school at the minimum leaving age. If educational opportunities were granted according to need, the reverse would, of course, be true. Moreover it is probable that the balance, in primary education at least, will be tipped further towards more able children in the future.[33] It is a fallacy to argue that the nation's economic and productive future depends on encouraging the most able and ensuring a full higher education sector if this is done at the expense of the less well able.[34] Currently post-school education is dominated by the higher education sector. If some of the difficulties of those without educational qualifications are to be overcome, there is a need for an expansion of adult education to meet their needs. Some of those who did not fully utilise the educational opportunities that school provided may require a 'second chance', but for the educationally handicapped young person the concept of continued education would be more appropriate.[35]

Summary

Detailed questions were asked about further education and training courses taken since leaving school as well as on-the-job training. Only 9 per cent of the handicapped had taken part in any form of further education since leaving school. Over half the handicapped young people participating in further education were doing adult literacy courses. Twenty-one per cent of the non-handicapped had taken or were planning to take a further education course. There were significant differences between the two main sample groups in the quality of the work-based training they received. Disadvantage at work for the handicapped was complemented by disadvantage in training: they were much less likely than the non-handicapped to receive formal training or to get apprenticeships. The majority of the handicapped who receive no training were doing semi-skilled or unskilled jobs.

12

Physical, Behavioural and Mental Handicaps[1]

Previous research on handicapped young people has concentrated on the experiences and problems of particular groups of the handicapped.[2] One unfortunate effect of this is that while substantial research has been carried out on the blind, deaf and other physically handicapped groups, very little has been done on the problems of the largest group of special school-leavers. The notable exception to this was the work by Tuckey and her colleagues, but even here the constituent groups of the sample were described and analysed separately.[3] While not wishing to underplay the special problems of specific groups of young people, the research described in this book attempts to show that there were common employment problems faced by all those who had educational handicaps. This was possible to a certain extent, but as the vast majority of the handicapped young people in the sample which formed the basis of the research were ESN(M), their influence on the statistics for the whole sample was very significant.

The total number of all of those ascertained as handicapped in the NCDS were included in the sample, so a larger base-sample would have been needed to carry out in-depth analysis of the smaller sub-groups among the handicapped. It is possible, however, that the character of the minority groups within the 'handicapped' sample may have been obscured to some extent under the influence of the predominant group. On the other hand as some of the employers' comments in Chapter 10 indicated, the experiences and needs of the ESN(M) group may not have been given enough attention in the past. This chapter attempts to redress any possible imbalance by describing some of the experiences of the three smaller sub-groups: the physically handicapped, the maladjusted and the ESN(S). The latter were omitted from many of the analyses reported earlier because of the severity of their handicaps.

The physically handicapped

There were sixty-three young people with physical or sensory handicaps in the original NCDS sample. In response to the initial letter, fourteen people refused to take part and one young man was untraced. Of the remaining forty-eight, thirty-five were interviewed in person, and the parents of two other young people were interviewed.

The young people in this small group suffered from a variety of different handicaps and many had more than one handicap. Nine people were physically handicapped, but five of them also had other problems, for example, epilepsy or educational subnormality. The physical handicaps included heart disorders, spina bifida, spastic quadriplegia and paraplegia and limb deformities resulting from polio and leprosy. Seven young people had been ascertained as 'delicate' (four of them being asthmatic) and of these one was also ESN(M). There were four each of deaf and partially sighted people, and none of these were ascertained as handicapped in other ways. However, three of the five partially hearing young people were ESN(M) and one was physically handicapped. Finally there were two people with speech disorders.

Assessment using the three functional scales suggested that the group as a whole was less handicapped in self-care ability than in social communication and participation. Twenty-two out of thirty-five people said they had no handicap in the self-care items, and a further three had only slight problems; nine were moderately or more severely handicapped. However only ten of them had no problems on the social communication and participation skills scale; fourteen were slightly handicapped and eleven were moderately or appreciably handicapped.

Education

Of the thirty-five people in this group, five had attended ordinary schools; three had been in special units attached to ordinary schools and the majority, twenty-seven, had been at special schools (where half of them had been boarders). Very few had remained at school beyond the minimum age, thirty having left in 1974 at the age of 16 years. There were only two young people who remained in school until they were 18, and significantly perhaps, both of them were in ordinary schools. Only ten young people had taken any further education courses. Eight were people who had left school at the minimum age, and in fact three were on courses to complete their education (for example, learning to read and working for 'O' level examinations). In addition another young man was receiving a couple of hours a week private tuition in reading. The other subjects taken in further education courses were horticulture, accounting, catering, painting and bootmaking, as well as secretarial skills and office studies. Four of the ten courses were at colleges specifically for the handicapped.

Four people had been on some type of assessment course, such as those run by the Spastics Society, or Employment Rehabilitation Centre or other assessment centre. To complete the picture on education and training it should be mentioned that one young man was in a Borstal institution, and five people attended adult training centres or some other centre for handicapped people (where they might have received basic education and training). So comparatively few of the group received any extensive education after reaching the age of 16. But on the other hand, there were only eleven people who expressed any wish for further education or training, and four of these people had already taken courses. Almost half this group had been advised against taking their desired courses for health reasons. For instance, Terry wanted to train as a mechanic but his parents and the careers service advised against this because the strain would be too much for his weak heart.

Labour market experiences

Altogether there were twenty-three people who had held a job at some stage in the two years since leaving school. Analysis of the social class of each young person's *first* job showed that about half were in skilled work, often non-manual. However three people had held unskilled jobs. The social class of the jobs done by the physically handicapped was, in general, higher than those of the ESN(M). This may suggest that there was a greater lack of opportunities for handicapped people in the simpler, low skill types of work, making it particularly difficult for the ESN(M) young person with additional physical handicaps to find work. Certainly this proposition was supported by the data, which showed that of the twelve people who were described in the NCDS sample as ESN(M) (in addition to having physical handicaps), only four were in employment. A further three were in adult training centres, one in a Borstal institution and four were unemployed. (Amongst the twenty-three non-ESN people, seventeen were employed or in education, four were unemployed and two in centres for the handicapped).

Thirty of this group had left school in 1974, although one of these had been in full-time further education since then. Of the remaining twenty-nine, twelve had held two or more jobs and seven had never worked (this included four people who attended adult training centres, and one girl who had taken a course of full-time training).

The two major indices of labour market experiences used in Chapters 8 and 9 were combined to distinguish those with 'poor' experiences, where 'poor' indicated a comparatively high amount of unemployment or a high number of job changes. For the purposes of this analysis young people who had held three or more jobs or who had been unemployed for at least a quarter of the time since leaving school (that is, at least six months in two years) were designated as having 'poor' labour market experiences. Using these criteria we found that seventeen of the thirty-one people who had left further education were defined as having poor labour market experiences; two others were unemployed at the time of the interview. Some examples follow. Terry, suffering from a weak heart and partial hearing, worked in a small factory assembling parts for tanks. He had been in work seven months and prior to that had been unemployed for sixteen months. He was very dissatisfied with the work which was 'boring and repetitive' but 'at least it is a job'. He had attended interviews for twelve other jobs but was turned down because of his weak heart.

In contrast, James, who was partially-sighted, but not registered as disabled, had held seven jobs since leaving school, but had only had three months' unemployment. His first job as a trainee bootmaker lasted six months, and he felt 'pushed into it' by his careers officer. Having left this he took a brick-making job, but the work was too heavy for him (he had been involved in a car accident) and he left after a short time. Through the employment exchange he heard of a job in a food-packaging factory. This, too, was short-lived as his poor eyesight made him a slow worker. A job as a gardener in a private house lasted four months, and he left only when he heard of a better job as nursery-worker. He received training in horticultural studies at an agricultural college while in this job. On being made redundant, however, he took a job as a shop assistant, but left this to become a waiter. James was very unhappy in his work and would ideally have liked to be an electrician.

Health reasons prevented both these young men from getting or keeping work. There were other instances in which young people had suffered in this way. Elsie, who had a serious heart disorder, was taken ill at work and 'They dismissed me without really finding out about my illness'. However it was in only about half the cases studied that health reasons appeared to be the main reasons for losing jobs.

Degree of handicap

Twenty-two of the people in this physically handicapped group of thirty-five suffered no functional handicaps. Thus it was not too surprising that fourteen of the seventeen young people who were employed were not handicapped in this way. It is notable however, that four of the eight who were unemployed, were appreciably or more severely handicapped. None of the employed group, and only one of the five people in adult training centres, was so handicapped. Furthermore, all the employed group with stable job records were non-handicapped in terms of self-care ability. With regard to social communication skills the results were less clear-cut. Those in employment were equally likely to be slightly or moderately handicapped or to have no such handicaps at all. The unemployed were similarly spread across the range, whilst those in adult training centres tended to be more handicapped in this respect. Five of the eleven people with moderate or severe handicaps in social skills, attended centres for the handicapped, or were in a Borstal institution.

Malcolm suffered from spastic quadriplegia and hydrocephalus, with the result that he could not walk and had little use in his hands. On the functional scale of self-care he was rated as severely handicapped, although he had no difficulty in communication. Malcolm reluctantly left school at sixteen because 'The school didn't think I could stay a year longer'. During part of the two years since then he had been on an assessment course. However he had never worked, and he spent his time 'making ashtrays and paperweights and chess sets from moulds. I type and use the typewriter to write short stories. I watch TV of course, and read.'

Karen suffered from polio as a child, and was left paralysed in one leg. She was rated as moderately handicapped on the self-care scale, but had no handicap on the social skills scale. Karen spent eighteen months on a secretarial course on leaving school, and then worked as a shorthand-typist. She did not consider that her disability would cause any problems for her when seeking a job.

The maladjusted

In the third NCDS follow-up (at 16 years) there were sixty young people who were ascertained as maladjusted, but not additionally ascertained as educationally subnormal or as physically handicapped. As part of the current research thirty-two young people were interviewed, eight people having refused to take part, and a further fifteen having moved to new addresses which could not be traced. The remaining five either broke appointments, or refusals were made by other members of their family, or in two cases, the addresses were too remote to issue to interviewers.

The young maladjusted people in this group suffered from a range of handicaps. Many had been in trouble with the police, as can be seen by the number – ten of the thirty-two – who were living in community homes. Others suffered psychiatric disorders or came from broken homes or other disturbed backgrounds, according to information from their teachers or doctors. A few examples illustrate some of their problems.

Paul was involved in two stabbing incidents in his early teens. He subsequently stole two cut-throat razors from a school laboratory and was finally expelled from school, at the age of 15, after throwing a knife at a fellow pupil. Anthony appeared to be a very quiet, shy young man. He was described by teachers at the school for maladjusted children which he attended, as 'immature, depressed and introverted, with aggressive destructive tendencies turned-in on himself'. Brian lived in a community home. At the time of the current interview he was waiting for his case to come up in court: his brothers were apparently all in prison. He lived with his ex-stepfather (who had also been in prison) and this man's girlfriend, whom Brian disliked.

In the group of 'maladjusted' young people there were significantly more men than women, the ratio being twenty-nine to three. (In the NCDS sample at age 16, the male/female ratio was forty-nine to eleven). Very few of these young people were handicapped functionally. On the scale indicating self-care ability only two of the group were found to have any handicap and neither of these was severely handicapped. However, over one-third of the group (twelve people) were handicapped in social communication skills, but ten of these only slightly so.

Education

As stated, ten of this group of young people lived in community homes. A further thirteen of the thirty-two were at special schools for the maladjusted. Eight young people were at ordinary schools and the remaining person received home tuition for two days a week. It is interesting to note that the group contained six 'early leavers' who did not stay at school until the end of the last summer term. Indeed, two of these left, or were asked to leave, before they were sixteen. By far the majority of the group, (seven-eighths), had left school by the summer of 1974. Of the four who remained beyond this time, two stayed for less than a year, and the other two were still at school at the time of the interview.

Only a few attended further education or training courses, although many of the young people expressed a wish to do some such course. Eight of the thirty who had left school had taken courses; three of these were at a trade training school and two others were on day-release courses at technical colleges, as part of an apprenticeship. Only three young people had attended college in preference to working, taking courses in business studies; catering and electronics/computing. A large number of maladjusted young people *wanted* to take courses – only four out of the twenty-two who had not taken courses, said that the did *not* want to. For the most part the young people also knew what courses they wanted to do.

Employment

At the time of this research only four of the thirty-two were still in secondary or further education. Two-thirds of the rest were employed, and half of these (eight people) were in skilled jobs. The eleven people not working included two unmarried mothers. However, the current employment situation did not tell the whole story, since there were several instances of maladjusted young people changing jobs frequently. Seven of the young people in the labour market had held four jobs or more. Another boy had never worked. Only eight people had held just one job, and two of them were unemployed when interviewed. They were the most likely group amongst the handicapped, to have unstable employment records.

As with the analysis of the experiences of the physically handicapped the two factors – 'number of jobs' and 'proportion of time unemployed' – were used together to define those with 'poor' labour experiences. Using these criteria eighteen people (of the thirty-two) were classified as having poor job records. A few examples serve to illustrate 'poor' and stable labour market experiences.

Immediately after leaving school, Charles worked as a slaughterman, killing cows and horses. Within six months he had become bored with the work and he took another job, on the land, picking peas. This lasted only a month as he did not like the work and the pay was poor. With help from his father he obtained a labouring job with a demolition firm. After six months this temporary job finished and he subsequently decorated beach huts for a private owner, until there were no more to paint. Since then he had been unemployed for nine months. Andrew had a stable labour market history. He worked as a sales assistant in a department store – a job which he had taken immediately after leaving school two years previously. He was happy in his work, although he felt that he was unlikely to improve his position because he 'does not like to take responsibility'.

Receipt of careers advice appeared to be an important indicator of labour market experience for the maladjusted. It was found that those young people having most contact with careers officers or teachers were the least likely to have poor records – only four out of ten compared with six out of nine amongst the group with least careers advice. This result was probably linked with the other finding that five out of six early leavers had poor job records; since four of these had had no careers discussions. Job records were next analysed according to the social class of the first job held. The results showed clearly that the higher the skill the better the work record. Six out of the thirteen people who had held skilled jobs had poor records compared with ten out of thirteen who had held semi-skilled or unskilled first jobs.

The educationally severely subnormal (ESN(S))

In the NCDS the incidence of severe subnormality among 7-year-olds was found to be at least 2.4 per thousand, probably as many as 2.6 per thousand when untraced children, who were likely to be handicapped, were included.[4] The criterion used for severe subnormality was an intelligence quotient of less than 50 (or 'untestable'), those graded as idiots or imbeciles by medical officers, and mongols without IQ scores.

The NCDS included fifty-three young people who, by the age of 16, were considered by their local education authority to be in need of special education because they were ESN(S). Two years later, at the time of the present research, two of these young people had died, and two more could not be traced. The parents of the remaining forty-nine were approached by letter, and forty agreed to be interviewed. In another three instances, the parents had no contact with their severely mentally handicapped child (two of whom were in long-stay hospitals and one in a hostel) and so a member of the staff caring for the young person was interviewed. Altogether, information about forty-three young people was collected by means of a special questionnaire and this was supplemented by data collected two years before, during the third NCDS follow-up.

The sample included nine mongols and nine young people with cerebral palsy, in addition to ten people for whom no specific medical condition was diagnosed. Others were for example, autistic, hydrocephalic, microcephalic and epileptic. Two young people were blind, and one girl was partially sighted. This young lady was multiply handicapped, being also microcephalic, epileptic, physically handicapped and with speech difficulties due to a malformed palate. By asking the parents how easily the young person could achieve certain tasks, it was possible to gain some measure of their functional abilities: forty-two parents (or staff) felt competent to report on this. Almost two-thirds of the group were rated as severely or very severely handicapped in self-care, although four others suffered only slight difficulties. On the other hand, the same proportion were judged to be slightly, moderately or appreciably handicapped in communication and social skills. Their capacity for employment was judged as most limited, and one-third of the group was rated as very severely handicapped on this scale. The one person assessed as *slightly* handicapped in self-care was in fact also the only person holding a job.

The interviews indicated five types of situations in which these young severely mentally handicapped people might have been, at the age of 18: they may have been attending school; receiving basic training at an adult training centre; holding jobs in open, or sheltered, employment; living in long-stay hospitals, possibly with no structured occupational activities from day to day; finally, they may have spent each day at home. In practice the amount of choice as to which alternative a handicapped person followed, was limited. The analysis which follows looks at the young people in each situation, their reasons for being there, and their possible future.

School

The minimum age of school-leaving for pupils at special schools, as for all pupils, is 16. However, the Department of Education and Science recommends that some of the less mature mentally handicapped may benefit from schooling up to the age of 19, and from part-time education even beyond then.[5] At the time of this survey, when the young people were 18 years old, only eight of the forty-three (16 per cent) were still at school. Indeed, almost half of the group had left school at the earliest possible age. (The figure may have been even greater, since six parents were unsure of the date of school-leaving.) Furthermore, there did not appear to be any great desire, on the part of the parents, for their children to have remained at school. Only six parents of school-leavers had wished for prolonged schooling, and four of these were parents of young people who had remained beyond the age of 16, but who had had to leave school because of a lack of places.

Turning to the eight young people who were still at school it was found that four of these attended hospital schools. There were two boys in the group, and both were in hospital schools. It is interesting that there were three times as many girls as boys at school, for, as we shall see later, when it came to adult training centres the balance swings as far in the opposite direction. When asked what their child did at school all but one of these parents mentioned self-help activities, for example, feeding, housecraft or even cooking. Comments by several of the parents suggested that they considered the teaching of self-care skills to be important for their child. Two parents mentioned speech therapy, and one other voiced a need for such therapy.

In general, however, parents were satisfied with the help and training provided by the schools, despite the fact that some felt their child was too handicapped to benefit from any training. Five parents said that there was nothing they disliked about the school; the other three overlapped in their complaints. Two parents complained of the *lack* of segregation of the more severely handicapped pupils from the less handicapped, and the subsequent deterioration in behaviour. (This was a criticism put forward by other parents in the total sample, when asked about schooling, and altogether six parents had mentioned it). Two parents complained of the lack of communication between parents and staff. One of the positive qualities at school, mentioned specifically by four parents, was that their children were with other children like themselves with whom they could communicate and play. It is possible that this contrasted with their images of adult training centres as places where predominantly older mentally handicapped adults carry out routine contract work.

Parents were asked what discussions they had had with staff at the school, or with a careers officer, about their child's future on leaving school. Only two of the seven had been involved in any discussions: one parent had been advised by a careers officer that her daughter was making good progress at school and would benefit from staying on; the other (who was not a parent, but a hostel warden) had discussed the matter with a social worker and psychologist and had decided that his charge was not mentally ready for an adult training centre. In the sample as a whole less than half the parents remembered such discussions with the schools staff, and only four had talked to a careers officer. It was not clear why the rest of the parents decided to keep their children at school. In view of later discussions as to why young people attend training centres, it seemed that parents were just told that their children could stay on, and accepted this since the child seemed happy at school. Besides, as one mother said, 'The school has been a help, because it's the only break I'd had.'

Employment

In fact only one person was working at the time of the interview, but two others had worked at some stage. The employed young man had held his job as a gardener, for two years, and his parents hoped he would continue to do so. The others had gone into jobs as packers on leaving school. Both had enjoyed their work, but the young woman was made redundant after two months and the young man was forced to leave after six months when his mother fell ill and could not transport him to work. Transport can obviously be a problem for a severely handicapped person in open employment. Those in adult training centres may be picked up by special bus. The employed man was fortunate in that he was able to cycle and lived near enough to his job to be able to cycle to work.

The parents of all three remembered some discussions prior to the young people starting work; two had talked to a careers officer. But in all cases it was the parents who found the job; the professionals merely approved or disapproved of the action, afterwards. Why did the parents want their children to work? In two instances it seems likely that the parents wanted their children to be treated like normal young adults and to work in a normal working environment. One mother was adamant that her son could have coped in an ordinary school and that he could also have coped in open employment, in spite of discouragement from the professionals. The other mother lamented her unemployed daughter's lack of social contact with 'ordinary' people.

Severity of handicap may not have been the most important factor influencing whether or not a severely subnormal young person could do a job. One of the three here was appreciably handicapped in self-care ability and severely so in communication skills and in employment capacity. What may have been more important was the parent's attitude towards the young person and his abilities. Only three parents in the sample of forty-three felt that their children could work in open employment and these were the parents of the only three who had worked. However their attitudes may have been shaped by the employers' acceptance of their child. Seventeen other parents felt that sheltered work was a possibility, but half of the group felt their children could not cope with any form of work.

Adult Training Centre

For many severely mentally handicapped, adult training centres provide the main source of stimulation and social contact. This was the case with the sample of 18-year-olds: half were attending such centres full-time. This included the young man who had held a job for six months. One other had spent five weeks at an adult training centre, but disliked it and eventually refused to go. The activities carried out by the twenty-one people currently attending adult training centres included sub-contract work, mainly packing, (nine did this) handicrafts or woodwork (eight people), social training and sports activities (eleven people) and other odd jobs. According to the parents' accounts, only ten young people took part in more than one of these activities. It is recognised that the accuracy of this information depends on the amount of contact between parents and the staff of the centre. However, it is still surprising that less than half the parents mentioned contract work, in view of the importance of this type of work as stated in the *Model of Good Practice*.[6]

Parents were asked about any discussions they had had prior to their child leaving school. Half had talked to someone at the school, but four had discussed the matter with professionals, for example, social workers, outside school. However, there remained one-third of the group who could recall no such discussions. Seven parents said that the staff had advised them to send their children to an adult training centre, but in four cases the reasons given were somewhat negative: 'He will never be able to work', and cast a picture of the adult training centre as a last resort. Three parents claimed that they were just told that their children would be going to the centre, and similarly, three other parents said there was never any question and so they did not discuss the matter with the school staff. There was little impression that the adult training centre was presented as a logical stage in the progression from school to sheltered, possibly open employment, and this was further borne out by the fact that very few parents mentioned assessment or preparation for work as one of the tasks carried out by the centres.

Even when asked the more hypothetical question of what they would like to see their children doing, half the group were satisfied that the young person should be kept occupied. Less than one-third said that they would like to see the young person working, and two others desired independence and a full use of the children's capabilities. Given that so many parents seemed unambitious, or were encouraged to be so by professionals and the lack of alternative provision, it is not surprising that many severely mentally handicapped people do remain in adult training centres for most of their adult years.

In the group of twenty-two young people who were at adult training centres or working there were only six girls, and yet there was a higher proportion of girls than boys at school. These findings suggested that parents were more anxious for their sons than their daughters to work even though their earning capacity may be low. This would explain why almost two-thirds of the men in the sample were attending adult training centres, or in open employment, whilst only one-third of the women were thus employed.

Those at home

In our sample there were six young people who remained at home, but in only two cases were the mothers happy with this arrangement; other parents wanted places at school, adult training centre or in open employment. Only one mother had originally planned that her son should remain at home, but she felt that this was no longer in his best interests. Half this small group had been offered places at an adult training centre but had not wished to attend and another girl had been in open employment. The quality of life for those at home obviously depended both on the severity of their handicap and on their parent's (usually mother's) commitments. Of the six young people in this group, four were encouraged to take some part in the housework, for example, by washing-up or dusting. But it is in the area of social contact that these people may have suffered most. A mentally handicapped person travelling daily to an adult training centre will meet a succession of people, the bus conductor, instructors, fellow-trainees, possibly kitchen staff, and although the level of interaction may be low they do experience a change of environment and a wider circle of people. In addition the rest of society might benefit from contact with the handicapped person. Social contact for the handicapped person at home may be restricted to occasional trips to the shops and infrequent visits to relatives. In this group of six, only three people went out of their homes with anyone other than their parents, although all but one went on short trips with other family members.

The future is perhaps less certain in the minds of parents of these particular young people than is the case for those of the group attending adult training centres. One mother anxiously awaited a place in a special care unit for her son as she felt he was deteriorating since moving from his last school. Another young man was soon to start at a training centre and until his mother knew whether or not he would settle there, she had no plans for the future. Two mothers wanted jobs for their children, although one mother was sure her son would not be able to hold a job. Another mother could not visualise a future different from the present. Only one girl apparently had her future assured – her brothers and sisters had agreed to care for her – and she would be happy continuing as at present, playing records and watching TV.

Those in hospital

This category overlapped with the previous groups. We have already mentioned young people in hospital schools, and in theory hospital patients may attend adult training centres; in this small sample none did so. There were eleven young people in residential hospitals. Apart from the four who attended schools, only one of the remainder appeared to be involved in any organised activity during the day, in this case occupational therapy. Parents' accounts of their children's daily lives included such activities as 'twiddling his thumbs', 'wandering about in the lounge' and 'playing about'.

Two-thirds of this group (seven people) had been in hospital since before they were 7 years of age. All but one of the group were in hospital by the age of 14. Why were these young people institutionalised in the first place? It was clear from the comments of most parents that they felt they could not cope with handling a severely mentally handicapped child, and in at least two cases the children were rejected by their parents. However it was distressing to find that one-third of the group (four parents) would have preferred some other type of care had it been available. One mother described how she was given twenty-four hours to decide whether or not to send her child to the hospital school; she could not afford a place in a private school, and no other placement was available. Two other parents had wanted places in CARE villages or Rudolf Steiner homes. Another father could remember little discussion before his daughter's admission to hospital, but added 'We did not realise it was a mental hospital'.

Ratings of handicap using the functional scales of assessment revealed that all these young people were the most severely handicapped group in the whole sample. However, there were individuals in the other groups who were as severely handicapped. Most of this group were severely or very severely handicapped on all three functional scales. As has been argued elsewhere these young people may be in hospital because of the severity of their handicap and at the same time their handicap may be made more severe as a result of institutionalisation, which may not encourage the acquisition of self-care skills.[7] Alternatively, in view of the fact that only two parents visited their children more frequently than weekly, and few of the young people ever came home for visits, it might be argued that parents may be out of touch with their child's abilities. There is evidence to suggest that the situation cannot simply be explained by any one of these factors.[8] It is not surprising, but nevertheless sad, that none of these parents had any hopes for the future, except that the young person would stay where he or she was.

13

Home and School and the Transition to Work

In addition to the main study of 18-year-olds, information was collected from the parents of those in the sample. Previous research had demonstrated clearly the important relationship between parental aspirations, attitudes and interest in school work, and their children's educational attainment.[1] As with the proportion of time spent in work, parents of those handicapped young people with very stable employment records were more likely to have been very interested in their child's progress (20 per cent, compared with 7 per cent of parents of the unstable). What did parents think of the advice and other help that their children had received whilst at school and when looking for work?

To find out, a brief questionnaire was constructed. In order to keep costs down, interviewers were expected to complete this short questionnaire only if the young person was living with his or her parents and if one parent was available to be interviewed. Altogether 389 'parental' questionnaires were completed – nearly two-thirds of the issued sample (excluding the ESN(S) for whom the 'parental' questionnaire was not used). As well as information collected from parents in this project there was background data available from the previous NCDS follow-ups. These provided data on some of the chief social characteristics of the parents.

Social class, education and aspirations

Only 23 per cent of parents of handicapped young people were in non-manual social classes when their children were sixteen, compared to 41 per cent of the non-handicapped.[2] The proportions of the special help and would benefit group parents who were in manual classes were similar to that of the handicapped group: just over three-quarters of the former and four-fifths of the latter. The difference between the parents of the handicapped and those of the non-handicapped in the extent of their schooling was almost as wide as the difference between their social classes. Parents were divided into two groups: where one or both parents left school after the age of fifteen and where both left before fifteen.[3] Forty-six per cent of the parents of handicapped young people were in the first group and 53 per cent in the second. The comparative figures for the non-handicapped were 55 per cent and 45 per cent. Fathers of the non-handicapped were much more likely to have left full-time education after the age of eighteen.[4] This trend depended in part on the age of parents, with older parents (who were more likely to have handi-capped children) having left school when the minimum leaving age was fourteen years.

At the follow-up of 16-year-olds in 1974, parents were asked to say into which of twelve ranges their *net* income fell.[5] Fourteen per cent of the parents of handicapped young people had net incomes of less than £20 a week, compared with 10 per cent of the non-handi-capped (9 per cent of the special help and 16 per cent of the would benefit groups).[6] The proportion of parents of handicapped young people who had net incomes under £10 a week was twice that of parents of the non-handicapped.

At the other end of the income distribution variations were less wide: 32 per cent of parents of handicapped young people had net incomes of £50 or more each week compared with 38 per cent parents of the non-handicapped. So the parents of handicapped young people, in general, were in lower social classes than those of the non-handicapped. They were also more likely to have left school at an earlier age and to have slightly lower incomes than parents of the non-handicapped.

Parents' aspirations for their children

The aspirations of handicapped young people in this study were very low (see Chapter 6). Previous research has shown that parents may have high aspirations for their children, regardless of whether or not they have the abilities to fulfil them. According to Carter: 'This is particularly noticeable with the less able children from middle-class and aspiring middle-class homes (the newly affluent), and especially with regard to sons.'[7] As Carter also notes, if these aspirations are not fulfilled, the boy's sense of failure may be aggravated and his home life become strained.[8] What sorts of jobs did parents desire for their children before they left school? Table 13.1 shows that the parents of non-handicapped young people were very significantly more likely to desire professional (nearly four times) and clerical (three times) jobs for their children than the parents of the handicapped.

TABLE 13.1   *Type of work desired by parents (%)*

| | Sample group | | | |
Type of work	Handi-capped[a]	Special help	Would benefit	Non-handi-capped
Farming, forestry, agriculture	6.3	6.1	3.3	2.8
Artistic	0.4	0.0	0.0	2.8
Professional, managerial	7.1	13.6	5.0	26.7
Service	11.8	15.2	16.7	7.6
Clerical	5.0	9.1	8.3	16.2
Manual industrial	31.5	28.8	40.0	20.0
Armed forces, merchant navy	2.1	7.6	5.0	5.7
Craftsman	2.5	0.0	5.0	1.9
Other[b]	33.2	19.7	16.7	16.2
Total	100	100	100	100
Number	238	66	60	105

$X^2 = 59.2$, 15 degrees of freedom, $p < 0.001$.

[a]   Includes ESN(S).

[b]   Includes those too vague to classify; adult training centre; sheltered work.

The differences shown in the Table 13.1 were not unexpected since previous research had indicated that aspirations are highest among parents in non-manual work and parents of those who go to grammar or independent schools (17 per cent of the non-handicapped were in grammar schools at 16).[9] These parents were expected to be better-off, provide the best facilities for study, have reached a higher level of education and have more evidence of reading activities in their homes than parents of children from other types of school.[10] The importance of parental aspirations to the success of young people at school must not be underestimated. One of the main claims from the Plowden Survey was that parents'. aspirations for their children had a stronger relationship with the child's achievements than any of the other characteristics of the home and school that were studied.[11] Parents of handicapped young people were unlikely to urge their children to the peak of their academic ability in order to fulfil their own ambitions and were less likely to be able to provide the environment to enable them to do it. On the other hand, parents of the non-handicapped had higher aspirations, which of course partly reflected the greater abilities of their children, but this is also in part self-fulfilling, since they were able to provide the encouragement and environment for the attainment of aspirations.

A large proportion of the handicapped faced inevitable 'failure' in employment, that is, low status work and underemployment. This prognosis was not counteracted by parental desires for higher status jobs for their children and the encouragement of success. If the education and employment systems do not provide facilities for the realisation and active promotion of higher aspirations and achievements by handicapped young people, there is little that parents can do in isolation and in the absence of job opportunities, they merely reinforce the inevitability of this failure.

Household type and social class

Surprisingly few of the sample of 18-year-olds had left home to live on their own (it was noted in Chapter 2 that the group that had left home were more difficult to trace and therefore a larger proportion were not included in the study) and their parents were therefore likely to be in close touch with the problems they had encountered and were tackling in their first two years in the labour market. The handicapped were more likely than the non-handicapped to live alone or to live in families with four or more children. Differences in household composition between the two groups were statistically very significant.[12] Amongst the handicapped nearly one in five of the ESN(M) and physically handicapped were living with only one parent. On the other hand 17 per cent and 11 per cent respectively came from households consisting of parents plus 4 or more siblings. One-quarter of the maladjusted young people had no male head of household.[13]

As well as seeking information about other members of the young person's household, data was collected on the employment of the head of the household (usually the father). This meant that a more up-to-date picture of social class could be drawn than that provided by data from the third NCDS follow-up reported earlier. The proportion of non-handicapped young people from households where the head was social class I (professional) was three times that of the handicapped (7 per cent as against 2 per cent); the proportion in intermediate or skilled non-manual classes was also three times that shown by the handicapped group (29 per cent against 10 per cent). At the other end of the social class scale the proportion of handicapped young people from social classes IV and V (semi-skilled manual and unskilled) was one-and-a-half times and twice that for the non-handicapped (16 per cent against 10 per cent and 10 per cent against 5 per cent). The widest variations between handicapped and non-handicapped young people, however, were in the proportions from households whose heads were not currently in employment. Fifteen per cent of the handicapped and 2 per cent of the non-handicapped were living in households where the head was unemployed. These differences were statistically very significant.[14] In addition, 8 per cent compared with 5 per cent were from households whose head was retired or sick.

Parental attitudes to school and work

In the study of parents, one of the first questions they were asked was whether there were any subjects or examination they had wanted their child to take at school but which they had not been able to take. Thirty-seven per cent of parents of handicapped young people compared with 24 per cent of non-handicapped mentioned such a subject or examination (the figures for the parents of the special help group and would benefit group were 25 per cent and 37 per cent).[15] This suggested that the parents of handicapped young people, who of course were predominantly from special schools, were less content with the composition of their children's education than parents of the non-handicapped. Parents of handicapped young people most frequently mentioned the following subjects: reading, writing and spelling, more academic courses such as English or history and vocational, domestic and recreational subjects.

When parents were divided according to social class (on the basis of data collected at the third NCDS follow-up) into manual and non-manual groups, some of the differences can be explored.[16] Equal proportions of parents of handicapped young people in manual and non-manual classes did not name any subjects. More parents in manual classes wanted practical subjects and more parents in non-manual classes wanted academic subjects. Eight times the proportion of non-manual as manual parents wanted academic subjects for their children. Parents in manual classes were twice as likely as those in non-manual classes to have wanted practical subjects, while similar proportions wanted reading, writing and spelling (5 per cent of non-manual compared with 7 per cent of manual).

Extra help needed

Next parents were asked whether the child in question had needed any extra help with lessons when he or she was at school but which he did not get.[17] The parents of handicapped young people were more likely than the non-handicapped to have wanted extra help for their child, again in the most basic subjects such as spelling, writing and reading (23 per cent compared with 1 per cent of the non-handicapped). The proportion of parents of the non-handicapped who said that extra help was needed in academic subjects was nearly twice that for parents of the handicapped (15 per cent and 8 per cent). Just over half the parents of handicapped young people compared with seven-tenths of parents of the non-handicapped said that no extra help had been needed. There were variations among parents of handicapped young people according to social class. Forty-six per cent of non-manual and 59 per cent of manual parents said they had not wanted any extra help for their child.[18] More parents in the non-manual than manual classes said that their child had needed more individual attention (8 per cent and 4 per cent), more had wanted help with maths or English (12 per cent and 3 per cent) but fewer said that their child needed help with reading, writing and spelling (12 per cent and 25 per cent).[19]

Advice on jobs or further education

It was shown in Chapter 7 that parents were an important source of information about jobs, but how happy were they with the advice that their child received from school about further education and jobs? Nearly three-fifths of parents of handicapped and non-handi-capped young people were happy with the advice their child had received.[20] When the rest were asked why they were not happy about the advice their child had received from the school, working class parents of handicapped young people were inclined to be most critical: 5 per cent of non-manual and 15 per cent of parents in the manual class said that their children had received no help or support. Amongst parents of the non-handicapped, however, it was the non-manual who were most unhappy.

Staying at school beyond the minimum leaving age

Did parents want their children to stay on at school after 16? Parents of non-handicapped young people were much more likely than others to say 'yes', and less likely to say that it was up to the child. The proportions were 35 per cent and 19 per cent compared with 22 per cent and 8 per cent of parents of the handicapped. The propor-tion of parents of handicapped young people who did *not* want their child to stay on beyond the age of 16 was nearly twice that for the non-handicapped (63 per cent and 26 per cent). These differences were statistically very significant.[21] The parents of physically handi-capped young people were most similar to the parents of the non-handicapped in their attitude to school-leaving and parents of the ESN(M) were least likely to have wanted their child to stay beyond the age of 16.[22]

These findings were at variance with those of the Plowden sur-veys. About 75 per cent of parents in 1964 had wanted their child to stay on beyond the statutory leaving age, 60 per cent in 1968, and by the end of the child's fourth year, up to 75 per cent again.[23] The main reason for the difference in findings must lie in the time period between the two surveys. Both the Plowden surveys of parents were carried out before the school-leaving age was raised to 16, and while the children were still at school, whereas this follow-up of NCDS families took place *after* the raising of the school-leaving age and after the majority of the young people concerned had left school. There was also, of course, the difference in the construction of the samples, and the questions used. More parents in manual occupa-tions said that their children were better off at work and more non-manual parents wanted their children to take examinations. Parents who had themselves stayed at school beyond the minimum leaving age were more likely to have wanted their children to stay on at school. Twenty five per cent of such parents of the handicapped had wanted their children to stay at school, compared with 20 per cent of parents who had left before the age of fifteen.[24]

Sources of advice about jobs

If the period of transition from school to work was a difficult one for young people, it was no less so for many of their parents. They were asked where they would seek advice about the young persons' future if they needed any.[25] Nearly one-quarter of parents of the handicapped and just over one quarter of parents of the non-handicapped did not know. Similar proportions of the special help and would benefit groups did not know where to seek advice. In addition, 5 per cent of parents of the handicapped said they had no-one to ask. A further 5 per cent and 2 per cent of the non-handicapped said they would leave it to the young person.

Altogether approximately two-fifths of both sets of parents said they would seek advice from 'official' sources (careers officer, school, department of employment, probation office or social services). Equally small proportions of both groups would have relied on friends. Five per cent of the parents of the handicapped group said they would go to their children's employers compared with 12 per cent of parents of the non-handicapped. Finally 14 per cent and 16 per cent respectively said they would not need to go anywhere for advice. None of the non-manual handicapped young people and 20 per cent of manual parents said that they would rely on themselves for advice; 19 per cent of the former compared with 4 per cent of the latter would leave it to the child and 9 per cent and 20 per cent said they would go to the social services.

Handicaps to employment

As well as general questions aimed at all parents there were three intended specifically for parents of the handicapped. Ninety-three parents of young people classified as ESN(M) were interviewed. When asked whether they thought their sons or daughters had a handicap which would make it difficult to get a job, 56 per cent said the young people were handicapped in this respect, and 44 per cent said there was no handicap. Forty-six of those who were 'handicapped' according to their parents and forty of those who were 'not-handicapped' had been interviewed personally. A comparison of the *functional* assessments of handicap within the two groups, suggested that the 'not-handicapped' group were indeed functionally less handicapped. There were differences in the amount of unemployment experienced in each group; 37 per cent of the 'handicapped' group were unemployed, and a further 13 per cent were attending an adult training centre. Seventeen per cent of the 'not-handicapped' group were unemployed and none had attended adult training centres.

In terms of having a job, the group defined by their parents as 'handicapped' were on the whole those who were least successful. A little surprisingly then, almost half of the employed 'handicapped' people had been in the same job continuously for almost two years, with no unemployment. Of the 'not-handicapped' young people twelve out of thirty-three employed people had worked continuously in one job since leaving school.

Changes to help the handicapped young person

Those parents who expressed the opinion that their children were handicapped were asked additional questions about changes they would like to see made, to help their children at school or in work. On the whole the parents of those young people with physical or sensory handicaps seemed less dissatisfied with the support available for their children, than were the parents of the ESN(M). Over half of the parents of the fifty-two ESN(M) young people were unhappy with the support their child had been given, and over half of those directed their criticisms against the school. In particular the need for improvements in teaching basic literacy were emphasised; 'because we won't always be here to help' as one parent explained. Various remedies to help in teaching were suggested – more patience with slow learners, more discipline; smaller classes, grouping children with the same problems all together and 'extra' help were all mentioned. Help at an earlier stage might also have improved the situation: one mother complained that her son was 9 years old before anything was done. Another parent, whose son was growing increasingly embarrassed by his lack of reading ability, would like to have seen a special tutor to help to overcome this problem.

An important part of their criticism was that of the lack of support *after* formal schooling ended, and two parents felt that courses for the mentally handicapped would improve matters. 'I would like to see the local authority and adult education systems tailored to take account of people like Graham. He seems to be in a no-man's land, not being physically handicapped, because mental handicap is not considered. There is no machinery for dealing with it.' It was felt that such courses would also have helped to alleviate the boredom of those mentally-handicapped young people who had been unable to find work. Many parents felt there should have been more advice available, and more effort put into finding work for their sons and daughters. 'Some form of preparation two months before leaving school' was the suggestion of one parent, whose son had been shown around only one factory.

Employer's attitudes

When it came to the subject of employers, almost two-thirds of the parents of the ESN(M) group felt that employers were 'just not interested' in the handicapped. 'They are in the business to make money, not to look after handicapped people.' 'They just want their work done.' As a result, it was felt, they did not give slow learners a chance, and a young person's chances of getting a job might disappear if the employer found that he had attended a special school. Parents said that employers lacked understanding of young people who could not read or write even though 'they are good physical workers', and would take the easier option of employing a literate person. 'There's always signs and notices to be read. Employers would rather have someone who can read, so they don't have to keep watching', but 'even if you can't read and write you can do a good job'.

As with the ESN(M) it was felt by parents of those who had physical or sensory handicaps that employers did not want the responsibility of employing a handicapped person, especially when there were so many non-handicapped applicants for jobs. 'They want five O-levels to lick stamps!' About half this group of parents felt that employers did not understand the problems of the physically handicapped. One mother related how her epileptic daughter had 'nearly got two or three jobs, and as soon as they find out she's got a disablement card they say they have no satisfactory work for the disabled'.

Financial problems

One-quarter of the parents of the ESN(M) said they had experienced financial problems. Often these resulted from the young person being unemployed (or earning pocket money only at an adult training centre). A few parents mentioned the expenses of visiting young people who had attended residential schools. Two parents suffered hardship in trying to clothe their son and daughter both of whom were now very large; one girl who was still putting on weight needed size 26 for clothes. Another parent had paid for a private tutor to teach her son. Over half the parents of the physically and sensorily handicapped said that they suffered financial problems as a result of the young person's handicap. Increased travelling costs to visit schools or hospitals were mentioned by six parents. Two parents had to pay for prescriptions for pills. Buying clothes for an epileptic girl who fell frequently, washing for a girl with a urine bottle, heating for a boy susceptible to the cold, and special lessons in syntax for a boy with communication difficulties were other financial burdens that had to be met. Only one parent mentioned the cost of having to look after an unemployed young person who was receiving only supplementary benefit, perhaps because this was too readily accepted as a family duty.

TABLE 13.2 *Type of school at age 16 (%)*

Type of school	Sample group			
	Handi-capped[a]	Special help	Would benefit	Non-handi-capped
Special school	61.5	0.0	0.0	0.0
Special unit	2.8	1.4	0.0	0.0
Home tuition	0.8	0.0	0.0	0.0
Community home	4.4	1.4	0.0	0.0
Hospital school	3.6	0.0	0.0	0.0
Comprehensive	11.5	42.0	48.1	53.1
Secondary modern	13.9	42.0	40.7	26.4
Grammar	0.8	8.7	7.4	16.8
Other	0.8	4.3	3.7	3.5
Total	100	100	100	100
Number	252	67	54	113

[a] includes ESN(S).

The young persons' schools

The vast majority of the sample left school in the summer of 1974. Table 13.2 shows the kinds of school attended at the age of 16. The proportions of young people who were day-pupils varied between 99 per cent of the non-handicapped and 50 per cent of the maladjusted. Among the handicapped groups 50 per cent of the maladjusted, 24 per cent of the ESN(S), 43 per cent of the physically handicapped and thirteen per cent of the ESN(M) were boarders at 16 years old.[26]

As well as collecting information from parents and employers it was thought that a fuller picture of the young persons' background would be gained by writing to a small number of headteachers. Some of the views and details they gave about facilities provided at their schools are documented in the rest of this chapter. Schools were selected from those attended by members of the sample at the age of 16. As the number of young people who attended special units in ordinary schools was very small a higher proportion of these were included in the sample than was justified by stictly random sampling. The other types of schools – special ESN(M) schools, other special schools and ordinary schools – were selected in order to give a broad geographical spread and to include both day and boarding schools. The final distribution of schools was as follows:

Special schools for physical handicaps (including severe subnormality)	18
Special schools for ESN(M)	18
Special units in ordinary schools	5
Ordinary schools	20
Total	61

Completed replies were received from fifty-three schools – a response rate of almost 90 per cent. Of the replies received twenty-two were from schools for the ESN, four from special schools for maladjusted children and five from schools catering for other handicaps. The rest of the schools who replied were non-special schools. I have called them 'ordinary' but they had special units for handicapped children attached to them and eight had handicapped children on their registers. For example, one 'ordinary' school had amongst its pupils one partially sighted girl, nine with only partial hearing, four epileptics, four with heart defects and a number of delicate children. Many of the schools which catered primarily for educational subnormality also had pupils with additional problems – physical handicaps, epilepsy, and maladjustment being the most common.

Contact with parents

Headteachers were asked which of four methods they used to keep in touch with parents. The four methods were: informal meetings at school functions; open evenings; careers evenings; invitations to attend the pupils' interview with a careers officer. This last alternative was used by all but five schools, although it is not known to what extent parents accepted the invitation. There were wide variations between different types of school in the provision of careers evenings. These were arranged by nineteen of the twenty-two ordinary schools, but only two special schools held such events. Furthermore less than half the special schools had open evenings, compared with nearly all of the ordinary schools. Overall the non-special schools used more of the four ways listed in the question, and two of the special schools in fact used none of the listed methods. Amongst the thirty-one special schools only one (ESN) used all four means, as compared to twelve of the other schools.

However, the special schools, and particularly the ESN schools, were more likely to contact parents in other ways. For example, five ESN schools allowed parents to visit at any time, and two schools held interviews for parents and staff. In two special schools, but in none of the others, staff visited parents at home. The different approaches arose in part from the fact that some of the special schools were residential which could cause problems when parents had to travel long distances: one school complained that its pupils were drawn from nine different local authorities. On the other hand contact in some residential schools was actually increased because staff met parents regularly on visiting days.

On the whole the situation in the ESN schools appeared to be more flexible – 'Parents are free to visit anytime' – than was the case in the ordinary schools, where 'Interviews are arranged as required'. Arranging interviews suggests that there has to be a definite purpose behind the parents' visit and does not encourage more casual enquiries. A greater proportion (55 per cent) of special schools had a high amount of contact with parents than was the case with ordinary schools (33 per cent). However, only four schools contacted less than 25 per cent of parents, and three of these were schools for ESN(M).

At the third NCDS follow-up teachers were asked whether they had met the parents of the child concerned during the last school year. Very significant differences emerged between the sample groups.[27] It was likely that both parents of any physically handicapped young person had attended a meeting.[28] This was also true for the parents of maladjusted and non-handicapped young people. But it was unlikely that both parents of the ESN had attended. For those parents who had met their child's teacher, there were also very significant differences in the originators of the meeting.[29] In the case of ESN(M) young people and to a lesser extent, the maladjusted, it was *the parents* who had prompted the meeting.[30] The proportions of parents who had not met teachers were: 28 per cent of parents of the physically handicapped, 50 per cent of those of the ESN(M) and 43 per cent of the non-handicapped.

Careers teaching

Headteachers were asked whether there was a teacher devoted fully or part-time to careers education. Six schools (all of them special schools) had no such teachers, and only two of the special schools had a full-time careers teacher (6 per cent compared with 27 per cent of ordinary schools). Three of the schools with special units had part-time careers teachers, as did five of the ordinary schools with handicapped pupils and seven of the ordinary schools without handicapped pupils. In addition two of the ordinary schools with handicapped pupils had full-time careers teachers, as did four of the latter. In fact the variation between the schools was wide, so that one of the ESN schools had two full-time teachers and two part-time teachers involved in this type of work, but most schools had part-time careers teachers. Four ESN schools said that they had teachers devoted to preparing the leavers for the world of work.

In most schools pupils were taught about filling-in forms and interview techniques and had talks from a teacher on specific occupations. To a lesser extent there were talks and films on work as well as factory visits. Work experience was less widespread especially among ordinary schools, less than half of which had any 'work-experience' schemes (45 per cent compared with 60 per cent of special schools). One ordinary school was planning to start 'work experience' in 1977; a school for the partially-sighted had run an extensive scheme covering ten types of occupation, but this had lapsed because of the difficulties of insurance. There was also one ESN school which offered work experience within the school, that is, in the kitchens, the gardens, working with animals and making concrete blocks. Three schools mentioned Trident Schemes. Twenty-four schools, evenly spread across different types of schools, took part in link courses, and two others were negotiating such courses with local colleges.

Preparing pupils for the adult world

It was difficult to group together all the ways by which schools 'prepared' their pupils for adulthood. Headteachers clearly had different ideas as to which topics achieved this. The headteacher of a public school which one of the non-handicapped young people had attended replied: 'We hope all education is for entry into the adult world and every activity is geared towards it.' Other non-specific answers, such as 'All aspects of life after leaving school are covered', and 'Preparation for the adult world takes place in many ways in normal class time' made it difficult to assess the relative amounts of coverage by different schools. Eight schools (seven of them ESN) referred to leavers' courses, but further details were not always added.

Pupils going on to further education or training

This question did not refer specifically to handicapped pupils. Considering for the moment just the special ESN(M) schools it was found that only six of these twenty-two schools reported that pupils went on to further education. The proportions who did so were very small: 'One in the last five years'; '1 per cent'; 'Very few, mainly on two-year residential courses run by the National Society for Mentally Handicapped Children'. One of these schools, however, reported that 20 per cent of pupils carried on to do further education. Apprenticeships rarely provided an outlet and only six schools reported that any pupils took apprenticeships: again the proportions of leavers doing so were less than 5 per cent. Very few pupils from ESN schools went to other forms of training. Two schools mentioned adult training centres (although the emphasis on training in these centres is not always very great); an employment rehabilitation centre was listed by two other schools and one school sent leavers on 'a course for handicapped school-leavers unable to get work'. The situation in the other special schools was better, with a few children going on to higher education. One school for maladjusted boys had carried out a survey of 100 former pupils a few years ago. Of these, 5 per cent went to higher education, 5 per cent to further education, 9 per cent started apprenticeships and 7 per cent took other types of training.

Summary

First, a smaller proportion of parents of the handicapped were in non-manual classes than those of the non-handicapped – one in five compared with two in five. Secondly, more parents of the handicapped had left school before the age of 15 and more of them than parents of the non-handicapped had low incomes. Aspirations among parents of the non-handicapped were higher than those of the handicapped.

More parents of handicapped young people than of non-handicapped were dissatisfied with the education that their children had received – having wanted him or her to take subjects that were not possible. More parents of the handicapped wanted additional help in school, particularly for spelling, reading and writing. Parents of the handicapped were more likely than parents of the non-handicapped *not* to have wanted the child to stay on at school after 16. The majority of them felt that there was little point. The proportion of non-manual parents of handicapped young people who had wanted their child to stay on to take examinations was five times that for manual parents. Many parents felt that employers were 'just not interested' in the problems of the handicapped. Some parents also felt that there was discrimination against those who attended special schools.

Fifty-three headteachers from selected special and ordinary schools provided information about contact with parents, careers advice and preparation for the world of work. There was more contact with parents about their children's careers in non-special schools. Special schools were less likely to provide 'work experience' schemes. Special schools had fewer contacts with employers: geographical isolation and wide catchment areas were seen as barriers to contact with parents and employers. There was evidence from the headteachers that handicapped young people were feeling a greater effect from the decline in job opportunities than the non-handicapped.

14

Conclusion

Inequalities in employment experiences

This investigation of the employment and labour market experiences of a nationally representative group of 18-year-olds has demonstrated that handicapped young people are a severely disadvantaged minority. Some of the main dimensions of this disadvantage have, for the first time, been documented in detail. They had access to a very narrow range of jobs at a low level of skill; these jobs were often repetitive, unrewarding and were carried out in poor conditions. Furthermore these jobs were the most insecure and therefore handicapped young people were disproportionately affected by unemployment. The vast majority of those who took part in the survey were capable of entering open employment, but the proportion of handicapped young people who were underemployed since leaving school was *five times* that of the non-handicapped.

Two years in the labour market was obviously too short a period on which to draw conclusions about the relative achievements of the sample. But many of the handicapped 18-year-olds seemed destined to grow up disadvantaged and to remain unqualified and untrained. Since it is more or less certain that the predominant structure of opportunity and organisation of employment will not change dramatically in the foreseeable future, handicapped young people will continue to carry out low-skilled jobs at the bottom of the occupational hierarchy. Moreover, as there is evidence of a contraction in unskilled employment, more of the 'failures' of the educational system are likely to remain underemployed.

Despite the broad definition of handicap used in this research, handicapped young people are not the only ones who are at a disadvantage in the labour market or who are doing unskilled work. Therefore many of the comments made in this concluding chapter and throughout the preceding analysis may equally well apply to the employment situation of other disadvantaged groups. Moreover while the handicapped school-leavers face some special difficulties in the labour market, the extent to which they share common problems with other groups of disadvantaged young people must not be overlooked. Policies which fail to take account of such links are likely to be ineffective in the long term.

A discussion of 'policies' aimed at counteracting labour market disadvantage assumes that an adjustment of the system will follow from the demonstration of need and social injustice. However, much of the systematic disadvantage discussed in this book is incapable of solution by 'tinkering' or minor adjustment. The analysis has posed some fundamental questions about the nature and organisation of work in industrial societies. For example, who gets which job and why? In which groups' interest does the occupational structure operate? Which groups control access to the finely graded levels of that structure? Who decides what is produced and how it will be produced? Thus policies aimed at significantly changing the social division of labour market experiences, including the enormous inequalities between handicapped and non-handicapped in this study, imply major changes in the nature of our society, for example, in the way employment is allocated, in the role of the educational system, in the organisation of individual jobs and in the distribution of resources. Such changes rest on the political and social will to create a more equal society. More fruitful in terms of the likely possibilities for social change are policies which may ameliorate some of the worst aspects of employment and the labour market. This is the intention of the proposals put in the second part of this chapter, following a discussion of the social distribution of employment experiences.

Disadvantage and handicap

It has been argued previously that the disadvantage that handicapped young people suffer in the labour market result from a number of interrelated factors: social class background; educational ability and degree and type of handicap. The way in which these are perceived and treated by employers and other agents of the market are of particular importance. The day-to-day experiences of young people and older people alike are shaped predominantly by work – by the possession of a job and by the type and level of that work. The kind of work and the status that the young person and later his own family occupy, are determined in outline at least, prior to labour market entry.

Although there are important individual success stories, it is unlikely that many of the ESN(M) school-leavers studied will ever leave the factory shop-floor or the semi-skilled and unskilled grades, throughout their working life. Indeed they may be fortunate to remain continuously employed, because these levels of work are the most vulnerable to the effects of changes in demand and industrial restructuring.[1] Moreover, the financial effects of unemployment,[2] the greater likelihood of sickness and disability than in other occupational groups[3] and perhaps, long-term unemployment in their late middle age[4] coupled with the relatively poor provision for pensions and other fringe benefits for workers below skilled level, suggests that these handicapped young people are likely to experience further disadvantage and perhaps poverty in later life. Thus the disadvantage of educational handicap may well be as influential in shaping their life-style and experiences over the next fifty or sixty years as it was during their first two years in the labour market.

Although the research was conducted within a relatively short period after the statutory leaving age there was evidence that a firm social division of young people in the labour market had taken shape. While the sample of 18-year-olds covered four main groups comprising a continuum of educational abilities (as defined by the educational system itself) analysis was inevitably concentrated on the extremes of that continuum. Handicapped young people were five times less likely than non-handicapped young people to be working in jobs of a clerical type. Non-handicapped young people were much less likely than other groups to have jobs in the industrial manual sector. But even when handicapped and non-handicapped young people who were working in the same type of employment – industrial manual – were compared, the latter were three times more likely to be in engineering trades, particularly as apprentices.

While the social class of young people is in general low, because occupations are hierarchically structured on the basis of experience and qualifications amongst other factors, handicapped young people were three times more likely than the non-handicapped to be in semi-skilled and unskilled work. Not surprisingly therefore it was the handicapped young people who were most deprived in both objective and subjective aspects of work; they were more likely to have to work unusual hours in relatively poor working conditions and they were more likely to be dissatisfied and unhappy. Handicapped young people also felt less secure in employment than their non-handicapped peers. This was clearly related to the objective conditions of their (and often their parents') labour market experiences. Twenty-seven per cent of the handicapped, compared with only 4 per cent of the non-handicapped, had experienced unemployment since leaving school. Just over one-third of those unemployed were living in households whose head was also out of work. There was a clear social class and therefore occupational and regional bias in unemployment. The handicapped young persons' experience of worklessness was *not* confined to a short spell after leaving school. For a significant proportion *un*employment rather than employment was more likely to dominate this two-year period. Again, this underemployment was concentrated on young people who had worked in the industrial manual sector. Handicapped young people were more likely than other groups to have unstable labour market records, low incomes and relatively small savings.

There are gross inequalities between young people in the receipt of education. The majority leave school at sixteen while the small minority who stay on and go into higher education have disproportionately large resources devoted to them. On entering employment it was found that many handicapped young people were faced with a 'Catch 22' situation which effectively blocked their main avenue for social mobility. Training opportunities are generally related to the level of job entered, thus without educational qualifications it is extremely difficult to obtain more skilled employment. The rigid apprenticeship system for training skilled workers also reinforces this low-skill trap. Fifty per cent of the handicapped compared with 16 per cent of the non-handicapped received one day or less of 'training'; while one in ten of the former were given formal training, more than two in five of the latter received this, mostly in apprenticeships. The majority of the handicapped who received no formal training were doing semi-skilled and unskilled work.

The facts analysed in detail earlier and summarised here suggest that the handicapped are systematically disadvantaged at home, at school and most importantly, in employment and the labour market.

Social division of secure employment

Some previous research has concentrated on occupational choice[5] or the transition from school to work.[6] But while there are real problems for some young people on entering the new social setting of employment, the challenge that confronts society is not only to ensure the efficient transfer of young people through the first stage of employment but, because many of them are likely to stay in certain sorts of jobs for the rest of their working lives, there is the additional challenge to improve the quality of their work experiences, rather than attempt to get them to accept the conditions of unskilled labour and the barriers to mobility as immutable.

The concept of the dual labour market was introduced at the outset and referred to periodically. It is accepted that this concept does not fully represent the hierarchical structure of occupations and the variety of labour markets which provide recruitment to them, but this simplification *is* useful in distinguishing broad groupings. Thus jobs at the extremes of the occupational hierarchy may be grouped roughly into those that offer the possibility of advancement and those which are dead-end (those differences are of course determined primarily by skill-level). Jobs of the former type enable young people to embark on progressive careers while those of the latter do not. In general, but certainly not exclusively, the former are skilled level jobs and above, which provide training and the possibility of rewarding work, while the latter are unskilled and semi-skilled, with little or no training. There is therefore a broad duality of experience in the sense that some young people, including a large proportion of the handicapped have consistently very different labour market experiences to others.

Job instability was associated with low-skill employment. Those young people whose last or current jobs were in the industrial manual or building sectors were more likely than others to have unstable early labour market histories. Those with very stable records were more likely to be found in skilled non-manual employment and those with unstable records in unskilled labour. Handicapped young people were twice as likely as the non-handicapped to have very unstable records.

Certain jobs are by definition insecure, for example seasonal work, but it was argued in Chapter 7 that other forms of work also have 'de-stabilising' influences. Some forms of low-skill employment are called 'casual'; in others a tradition of fitful employment may have been created in a situation of fuller employment by the reaction of young people to low pay and poor working conditions. The stigma of unemployment may now be keeping young people in this kind of work rather than any attachment to the job. But these jobs are the very ones that are most affected in a recession. The background to this research was high and rising unemployment. Despite the fact that older workers suffer most from redundancy, the employment prospects of the young also deteriorate relatively to 'prime age' workers in a recession. Firms are liable to change their recruitment patterns at such times and those who change their jobs most frequently are more susceptible to unemployment. Moreover, recent unemployment has been largely concentrated on manual employment, reflecting a long-term decline in the demand for this labour. This reduction in the demand for unskilled labour by manufacturing industry falls heavily on handicapped young people. The unqualified are not only hit by the decrease in overall demand and the demand for labour in certain industrial sectors, but also by the process of 'trading-up' the recruitment market.[7] With an increasing pool of labour employers tend to take on those people with qualifications to do tasks previously done by unqualified people.

What is the role of employers in this social division of secure employment? Recruitment is not always 'formal', on the basis of qualifications or aptitude tests. This is particularly true for the low-skill jobs covered by the secondary labour market, where recruitment is often 'informal' with little more asked than 'how old are you? When can you start?' In this sector, good appearance and other visible personal characteristics are important in determining access to jobs. But handicapped young people often lack these characteristics. Thus while there may not be an open policy of discrimination against handicapped young people, this is what effectively happens when employers base their recruitment on personal qualities that may have little bearing on how well the young person can do a job. In addition the survey of employers (analysed in Chapter 10) revealed a more systematic policy of discrimination against certain forms of physical and mental disabilities, such as epilepsy. Regardless of how active or able a disabled young person may be, he is likely to experience great difficulty in finding work. Employers' perceptions of handicap were usually of physical impairment and they were therefore not aware of the special problems facing an ESN(M) or maladjusted young person. These young people were most likely to be classified as having unstable work histories, and they were most likely to react adversely to certain features of the employment situation. In the absence of an understanding of the special problems of these young people and of the need to improve work satisfaction, employers of unskilled labour are exacerbating their problems. Because some unqualified young people appear not to be interested in keeping a job for a long period, employers make no efforts to retain them by improving conditions, preferring instead to believe in a stereotype of fitful youth, uninterested in work, and they recruit young people on that basis.

Evidence from this study of 18-year-olds suggests, therefore, that a significant section of school-leavers are faced with a restricted pattern of access to employment, and, at that, restricted access to employment of the lowest skill level. Many handicapped young people appear to be at a disadvantage even within the secondary labour market. Thus they may be said to form an *underclass* lodged at the foot of the occupational structure, a sub-set of the secondary labour market. Whether this hypothesis is correct and if so, the permanence of this status, must await the results of further research. However, it is clear from this study that an immediate and wide social division of labour market experiences and, because of the importance of employment, a social division of life chances, operates to the disadvantage of the handicapped.

Social distribution of disadvantage

Who were the most disadvantaged in the labour market? Differences in employment experiences were not based simply on physical limitations. ESN(M) young people were the most likely of all to be in the lowest occupational classes. Women were more likely than men to be less than fully employed. Some previous research has shown that young women are less worried than young men about unemployment,[8] which reflects perhaps, the fact that society in general appears to undervalue women workers. Young people (predominantly men) classified as 'maladjusted' at school were least likely to be fully employed. They also had the most unstable employment histories, followed by ESN(M) young people.

Those with functional incapacities; those who were mentally retarded at the age of seven; those who suffered from minor nervous complaints and those with behaviour difficulties at the age of 16, were the most likely to be underemployed and to have unstable work histories. While some of their minor nervous complaints were probably reactions to the trauma of unemployment and the rejection that entails, there was no doubt that some of the most disadvantaged were more sensitive and emotionally insecure than other young people. It does not follow from this of course, that they *deserve* to occupy a disadvantaged position in the labour market; rather there is a need for society to recognise their special problems and the social factors underlying their disadvantage. Underemployed young people were more likely than the fully employed to have been living in overcrowded accommodation when they were 16, to have fathers who were in manual occupations, to have left home or to have come from either single parent families or large families.

Clearly the social division of life chances does not begin with labour market entry. The social class of parents, determined primarily by their occupations, is crucial in shaping their image of society and their view of the child's education. Successive research studies over the last fifty years have demonstrated beyond doubt that family, class and education are closely interrelated.[9] It is well known that working class children are under-represented in higher education.[10] Even when children are of similar ability, they are far more likely than middle-class children to deteriorate in performance and to leave school at the minimum age.[11] Similar trends are found in many other advanced industrial societies.[12] There are important variations between working-class families in their home-centredness and careers orientations.[13] Therefore, as Dennis Marsden has pointed out, the essential fact is that: 'Parents guide their children's education by what they are, what they do consciously, and possibly more important, what they do unconsciously'.[14] The Schools Council inquiry into early (and therefore unqualified) school-leaving found that the great majority of parents of early leavers had themselves completed their own full-time education at the age of 14.[15] That inquiry showed that the fathers of the majority of these 15-year-old leavers were in manual occupations. The young leavers were likely to have been in large families in overcrowded accommodation. Similarly many parents of ESN children in special schools are in the lowest income groups.[16] Some ESN children have organic disorders and some defects which create learning problems, but for many their educational handicap is socially generated.

Parental background and class, home and neighbourhood, interruption of family life, the failure of schools to involve families and so on, may all contribute to learning difficulties. These young people and their families bear some of the social costs of others' affluence, some of the costs of the predominant organisation and aims of production. It is the employment situation therefore that has been demonstrated time and time again to have a most significant influence, through the mediation of their families, on young people of successive generations. The educational system formally divides young people into those groups which will enter the occupational structure at various stages. Educational qualifications help to facilitate the social division of employment; as Bosanquet has argued, improved and expanded education 'has been accompanied by a widespread reliance on academic qualifications as an important credential for sorting primary from secondary workers'.[17] This falls particularly hard on immigrant and older workers who lack qualifications, but also effectively discriminates against the pool of failures from the educational system.

Counteracting disadvantage in the labour market

Various policies aimed at ending the worst inequalities in labour market experiences and the disadvantage suffered by handicapped young people, have been suggested explicitly and implicitly by the preceding analysis. In this final section some of the most important ones will be summarised.

Education and disadvantage

Young people of different ages leaving educational institutions may be ranged on a continuum of success, based on qualifications. This continuum corresponds roughly with the occupational structure, ordered hierarchically in terms of pay, working conditions, responsibility, fringe benefits, security and so on. It would be entirely false to conclude, however, that this correspondence represents the reasonable outcome of a process which scientifically matches jobs to ability. In the first place this model assumes that abilities are fully realised. The education system is geared to the realisation of certain abilities, as demonstrated by examination results. It is primarily concerned with the escalation into further education. As a consequence special education occupies a low status in relation to the other sectors: it is separate and not part of the serious business of preparing young people for careers. In addition, there are good reasons why the abilities of some children are restricted – physical handicap and home environment for example – for which the educational system does not compensate. Some children have to leave at 16 because there is no provision beyond that age, others because their families cannot afford to maintain them.

Secondly, it has been demonstrated that employers may exert what amounts to a discriminatory influence on this apparently apolitical and unbiased matching process. Thirdly, young people do not all start from the same position, with the same life chances. Those parents with higher incomes and more secure employment can provide a more educational environment for their children. Thus, with some exceptions, the hierarchical structure is self-perpetuating. These are some of the reasons why the gross inequalities in labour market and employment experiences that have been analysed are so persistent over time.

Despite the findings of Rutter and his colleagues,[18] the educational system is limited to a great extent in its ability to influence the life chances of individuals. In Bernstein's words: 'education cannot compensate for society'.[19] Indeed focus on the educational system and families diverts attention from the system of production and the social relationships at the workplace, where these social divisions have their roots. Additional teachers, educational psychologists and social workers alone, although important in an overall strategy, will not significantly alter the life chances of handicapped young people; it is the labour market which has the major influence on their lives. However, as part of an overall strategy based on social justice there is a need to ameliorate those inequalities which the educational system *can* influence including those that it creates. This includes a greater concentration of resources on the least able pupils, even at the expense of the 'gifted'.

The purposeful introduction of Section 10 of the Education Act, 1976, would end the injustices of separate provision as opposed to special provision within an ordinary setting and begin to break down the stigma of handicap that is revealed in the work setting. Link courses in further education colleges should continue to be used imaginatively for those in special schools in the short term. Leaving ages should not be rigid, especially for handicapped young people. In addition, educational allowances should be paid to those staying on at school to provide for their maintenance and thus remove the financial barrier to continuing education.

Most importantly, the content of education and teaching should encourage young people to want to stay on, rather than reject it at the first opportunity. Those who argue that many young people do not enjoy education or do not have the capacity to profit from it, often fail to see that this may be a criticism of the organisation of education rather than individual failures. Indeed the fact that for many young people, including some of those in this research, education was an unpleasant experience is a sad indictment of the educational system. Reforms of education are always bitterly opposed by some groups. In the same way that employers and others opposed the extension of compulsory secondary education beyond the age of 14 sixty years ago, distinguishing 'the more promising' children who were mentally capable of benefiting from higher education and 'the less promising' children who were not,[20] there are likely to be increasing calls in the future for more 'relevant' education for those who leave at the minimum age. If such calls are heeded, this is likely to increase the differences between those who benefit most from educational resources and those who leave at the earliest opportunity.

Careers guidance and teaching

Careers advice alone will not significantly alter the labour market experiences of handicapped young people, but those who went straight from school into work were more likely to be fully employed than those who could not find a job or were sick after leaving school. Also practical careers guidance in schools seemed to have some effect on the transition from school to work. I have suggested elsewhere that the careers services for young people should be rationalised in order to facilitate adequate preparation for employment and a successful entry into employment.[21] This would entail the Department of Employment taking responsibility for placement and the combination of the functions of careers teachers and careers officers. The latter would be based in secondary schools and colleges, but would maintain contacts with local employers and would be administered by the Manpower Services Commission. This reorganised careers service could concentrate on preparation for work by arranging work experience, talks, films and visits and other practical guidance.[22] The Department of Employment on the other hand, could concentrate on placement, and in liaison with the careers service, make recommendations to government and employers on improving working conditions.

Regardless of any future reorganisation of the employment services for young people, evidence from this study shows that careers officers were unsuccessful in contacting significant groups of ESN(M) and maladjusted young people and suggests that special efforts must be made to work with them in an attempt to improve their employment prospects. Clearly it is crucial for their special problems to be recognised during the transition into employment, as they are in special education. But the process of preparation for employment must begin earlier, at least two years before leaving, if it is successfully to introduce young people to the realities of the labour market.

Further education

The simple act of leaving school does not diminish the importance of an individual's educational handicap, yet there is very little special provision for such young people beyond the age of 16. Only 9 per cent of the handicapped had taken part in further education, mostly adult literacy classes. But there was a large, unmet, demand for education and training, with just over two-fifths of the handicapped who had not taken part in further education or training saying that they would like to do so if given the opportunity. There is an urgent need to provide handicapped and non-handicapped people, both young and old, with a second chance in education. Experience in other European countries such as France, Sweden and West Germany could be used to provide young people leaving school with the right to a certain amount of study-leave or day-release courses. This system might also be extended to older workers who also missed out on the benefits of education at their first opportunity. Individuals might be awarded say, five years' worth of day-release credits which they may 'cash in' for courses at any time, on say, a basis of one course per year.

Employment

We turn now to the employment situation which must be the main focus of any serious attempt to counteract disadvantage in the labour market. Although unemployment is a major evil that demands a solution through the creation of permanent jobs, there is a danger that a preoccupation with unemployment will lead us to ignore the need to change the existing system of employment and to improve individual jobs. Moreover, in any policy to increase permanent employment, care must be taken to ensure that the social costs of unemployment are not shifted across the generations, through, say, early retirement schemes, but are shared amongst all groups, by, for example, a shorter working week. It is essential that permanent jobs are created which provide civilised working conditions, training and room for personal initiative and involvement. It has been demonstrated that many handicapped young people lacked persistence, were emotionally unstable and had low thresholds for boredom and frustration. The 'de-stabilising' aspects of some low-skilled jobs, for example, arduous labour, poor conditions, monotonous work and low pay, react with these personal characteristics and result in the young person leaving voluntarily or getting the sack. In a study carried out by the Clothing Economic Development Council into labour turn-over, boredom was the most-often-quoted *avoidable* reason why girls thought others might leave.[23] They also reported a gap in the knowledge of managers about shop-floor conditions and said that they were out of touch with the needs and aspirations of those on the shop-floor (especially the young).

In order to counteract the de-stabilising aspects of some jobs and provide handicapped young people with more job satisfaction it is necessary, first, to redesign many jobs. There have been a number of successful, though limited, attempts at redesigning jobs partly in an effort to increase job satisfaction.[24] One of the best known of these was carried out in the Philips factory at Hamilton.[25] The jobs of women assembling fan-heaters were enlarged so that each woman assembled a complete heater rather than one part of it on an assembly line. Thus they were involved with the whole object under production and with different procedures. In view of the young workers' need for social contact and support, one fruitful direction for redesigning jobs would, perhaps, be group work.[26]

Whilst in Great Britain there is the beginning of a long overdue advance on job-improvement and job-enrichment,[27] in the United States a considerable amount of research has been done on the rather difficult concept of 'job-development' and some helpful lessons could also be drawn from their experience. Job-development has been defined broadly as an activity concerned with finding jobs for the 'disadvantaged' or with attempts to help them retain jobs after placement.[28] It includes counselling, persuading employers and 'job-coaching' which entails supporting the worker in employment. The closest role in Britain to the job-developer is the Disablement Resettlement Officer. In America they claim most success with employers when job-development is perceived as a *manpower service*, that is, as a means of increasing company efficiency and reducing costs. 'When the employer views job-development as a 'job for the poor' strategy, he confines himself to job-pledges and opening job-slots for the disadvantaged at the entry level without any commitment to an examination and revision of the organisational structure and processes that continue to deny opportunities for the majority of the hard-to-employ.'[29] Thus, it is argued, the job-development unit should be perceived as selling a logic of manpower operation, not hard-to-place workers.

Ferman distinguishes three forms of job-restructuring.[30] Jobs may be *segmentalised* by breaking them into simpler tasks to fit the immediate talents of the hard-to-employ. They may be *enlarged*, by combining a series of tasks to produce a more interesting and mobile job unit. Thirdly, they may be *simplified,* for example, by altering the qualifications required to hold the job, such as educational achievement, or the training thought necessary for the job. Obviously it is not enough to know how to restructure jobs; employers and others must be persuaded to adopt these mechanisms. Trade unions, management bureaucracy, job-descriptions and traditional ways of doing tasks as well as possible initial increases in costs of supervision create a barrier of reluctance to initiate a job-restructuring programme. Unfortunately very little has been done, in this country at least, in experimenting with job-design and improvement and clearly the government will have to give a lead. For those who doubt the importance of such measures Lockwood has provided one obvious but powerful answer: 'the thought that, at the point of production, we "produce" among other things, human beings, is worth keeping in mind'.[31]

The second aspect of this strategy for counteracting disadvantage is job-training. Handicapped young people who had received formal training were more likely than those who had not to have stable employment histories. Training is important in two respects: it improves the skill of the individual worker and so the workforce as a whole, and it increases satisfaction with employment. It is semi-skilled and unskilled employment that provides least training. The unenacted parts of the 1944 Education Act could be implemented, making it compulsory for employers to give young workers day-release. The government could provide more resources, through the Training Services Division of the Manpower Services Commission and the Industrial Training Boards coupled with powers to compel employers to provide training for young people.

In other European countries training plays a much more significant role in the lives of school-leavers. In France, the length of apprenticeships has been reduced to two years full-time study on an integrated course of education and training. Those young people not following an apprenticeship are guaranteed the right to paid study-leave of 100 days per year. The West German government has declared its intention to confer education rights on *all* young people. Employers must have training skills and knowledge of teaching methods or else they must appoint a qualified training officer. A start has been made in this country with pilot schemes for vocational preparation by working in conjunction with education authorities, Industrial Training Boards and the Training Services Division, but the government must now take the initiative in training *and* job-development.

Careers officers in the proposed school-based careers service could act as 'job-coaches', helping young people and those who are handicapped in particular, with counselling and advice about different aspects of the work situation, including training opportunities. However training alone may create aspirations that cannot be met under the current structure of employment. Thus there is a need for more mobility between unskilled, semi-skilled and skilled groups. The apprenticeship system is a major barrier to mobility, providing access to skilled employment at only one stage of development. A shorter and more flexible apprenticeship that provides access at all ages, would increase skill mobility and enable the workforce to adapt more quickly to changing technology. Increased further education opportunities would also increase mobility into skilled manual and non-manual employment.

The third and final strand to this policy for improving the employment experience of handicapped young people is the education of employers. Whilst the enforcement of the quota scheme is important to preserve the employment rights of disabled people, it is difficult to discriminate positively in favour of the vast majority of handicapped young people because they are not visibly, or medically, impaired. It is important, however, to ensure that employers do not knowingly or unknowingly discriminate against the handicapped nor encourage a false stereotype of feckless youth which has the same result.

In contrast to disadvantaged workers Ferman has identified 'disadvantaged employers' who 'lack the necessary skills and talent to understand and appreciate the manpower problems of the hard-to-place workers. He holds certain stereotyped notions of what an individual or group can do and he is blind to alternatives or change.'[32] While this may apply to only a very small minority of employers, this research shows quite clearly that employers are not aware of the special problems of ESN(M) and maladjusted school-leavers and that they are unwittingly barring the access of some handicapped young people to jobs. In addition they are apt to make generalisations about the capacity for employment of some disabled people. Thus they tend to overestimate both the severity and inflexibility of certain kinds of disablement.

Trade unions obviously have an important role in the education of their members and of employers, and in the drive for improved working conditions. Their role is particularly important in improving wages for unskilled workers and ending the differentials created by age-related salary sacles which provide a positive inducement to employers to terminate employment. Unfortunately, however, there is little indication that they are any more aware than many employers of the special problems of the handicapped.

In the face of ignorance and possible resistance to change, particularly in a period when the supply of unskilled labour is plentiful, it falls to the government to provide a lead in a strategy to counteract disadvantage in the labour market and to ensure that every school-leaver has the chance to realise his or her full potential. The main focus for change in the first place must be the labour market: the creation of new jobs, opening-up the occupational hierarchy and redesigning monotonous and unrewarding work. Until such measures are enacted on a wide scale the fate of many handicapped school-leavers will continue to be underemployment and insecurity.

Notes and References

Chapter 1

1. Titmuss, R. M. (1974) *Social Policy* (London, Allen & Unwin) p.66.
2. Department of Education and Science (1978) *Special Educational Needs* (London, HMSO).
3. See, for example, Harris, A. I. *et al.* (1971) *Handicapped and Impaired in Great Britain,* vol. 1 (London, HMSO).
4. Reubens, B. G. (1970) *The Hard-to-Employ: European Programmes* (New York, Columbia University Press), p.126.
5. Walker, A. (1976) The hardest job, *Community Care,* no. 139, pp. 20–2.
6. Inner London Education Authority (1975) *Survey of Opportunities for School Leavers,* p.1.
7. Department of Education and Science, *Special Educational Needs,* p.41; Rutter, M. *et al.* (1970) *Education, Health and Behaviour* (London, Longman); see also Department of Education and Science (1975) *Integrating Handicapped Children.* (London, HMSO) p.3.
8. See, for example, Thorpe-Tracey, R. (ed.) (1976) *Integrating the Disabled: Report of the Snowdon Working Party* (Horsham, National Fund for Research into Crippling Diseases); Cope, C. and Anderson, E. (1977) *Special Units in Ordinary Schools* (London, Institute of Education). The concept of special education as separate full-time education in special schools and classes has been seriously questioned in recent years, and the policy of integrating handicapped children in ordinary schools has been embodied in Section 10 of the Education Act, 1976, though this is not yet enforced.
9. Department of Education and Science, *Special Educational Needs,* p.17.
10. Inner London Education Authority, *Survey of Opportunities,* p.2.
11. See Craft, M. and Miles, L. (1967) *Patterns of Care for the Subnormal* (Oxford, Pergamon).
12. National Union of Teachers (1975) *Educating the Handicapped* (London, NUT) p.73; Department of Education and Science *Special Educational Needs,* p.43.
13. Department of Employment (1977) 'Manpower planning: young people leaving school in Scotland and Great Britain', *Department of Employment Gazette,* vol.85, no.6, pp.600–62.
14. Department of Education and Science, *Special Educational Needs,* p.36.

15. Kelsall, R. and Kelsall, H. (1971) *Social Disadvantage and Educational Opportunity* (New York, Holt, Rinehart & Winston) p.2.
16. Passow, A. H. (ed.) *Deprivation and Disadvantage* (Hamburg, Unesco Institute for Education) p.16.
17. Liebow, E. (1967) *Tally's Corner* (London, Routledge & Kegan Paul).
18. Liebow, E. (1970) 'No man can live with the terrible knowledge that he is not needed', *New York Times Magazine*, 5 April; Marsden, D. (1975) *Workless* (Harmondsworth, Penguin) chaps 7–9; Sennet, R. and Cobb, J. (1977) *The Hidden Injuries of Class* (Cambridge University Press).
19. Walker, A. (1976) 'Justice and disability', in Jones. K, and Baldwin, S. (eds), *The Yearbook of Social Policy in Britain 1975* (London, Routledge & Kegal Paul).
20. Department of Employment (1980) Unemployment: summary analysis UK Table 104 *Department of Employment Gazette*, vol. 86, no. 8, p.978.
21. Ibid, p.908.
22. Department of Employment (1974) *Unqualified, Untrained and Unemployed: Report of a Working Party set up by the National Youth Employment Council* (London, HMSO) p.19.
23. Kalachek, E. (1969) *The Youth Labour Market* (Ann Arbor, University of Michigan).
24. Robertston, E. J. (1970) 'Local labour markets and plant wage structures' in Robinson, D. (ed.), *Local Labour Markets and Wages Structures* (London, Gower Press) p.16.
25. Ibid, p.28.
26. Doerings, P. B. and Piore, M. J. (1971) *Internal Labour Markets and Manpower Analysis* (Lexington, D. C. Heath) chap. 8; Doerings, P. B. (1974) 'Low pay, labour market dualism and industrial relations systems', in Organisation for Economic Co-operation and Development, (1974) *Wage Determination* (Paris, OECD) p.16.
27. Ibid, p.8.
28. Bosanquet, N. (1973) *Race and Employment in Britain* (London, Runnymede Trust).
29. Jones, P. *et al.* (1975) *All Their Future* (Oxford, Department of Social and Administrative Studies, Oxford University) p.37.
30. Ashton, D. N. and Field, D. (1976) *Young Workers* (London, Hutchinson).
31. Boudon, R. (1974) *Education, Opportunity, and Social Inequality* (New York, Wiley).
32. Lipset, S. M. and Bendix, R. (1959) *Social Mobility in Industrial Society* (London, Heinemann); Schorr, A. (1966) 'The family cycle and income development', *Social Security Bulletin*, February.
33. See, for example, Williams, W. M. (ed.) (1974) *Occupational Choice* (London, Allen & Unwin).
34. Beynon, H. and Blackburn, R. M. (1972) *Perceptions of Work* (Cambridge University Press).
35. Allen, S. (1975) 'School leavers and the labour market', *London Educational Review*, vol. 4, no. 2-3, p.65.
36. Titmuss, R. M. (1968) *Commitment to Welfare* (London, Allen & Unwin) p.159.

Chapter 2

1. See, for example, Carter, M. P. (1962) *Home, School and Work* (Oxford, Pergamon); Thomas, R. and Wetherell, D. (1974) *Looking forward to work* (London, HMSO).
2. Ferguson, T. and Kerr, A. (1960) *Handicapped Youth* (Oxford University Press).
3. Rhodda, M. (1970) *The Hearing Impaired School Leaver* (University of London Press).
4. Myers, S. O. (1975) *Where Are They Now?* (London, Royal National Institute for the Blind).
5. Tuckey, L. *et al.* (1973) *Handicapped School Leavers* (Windsor, NFER; National Children's Bureau Report).
6. Roberts, D. J. (1975) 'A survey of 235 Salford handicapped school-leavers for the years 1970, 1971 and 1972 compared with 235 non-handicapped school-leavers for the same years', *Public Health,* vol. 89, no. 5, pp.207–11.
7. Butler, N. R. and Alberman, E. D. (1969) *Perinatal Problems* (London, E. & S. Livingstone); Davie, R. *et al.* (1972) *From Birth to Seven* (London, Longman, in association with National Children's Bureau); Fogelman, (ed.) (1976) *Britain's Sixteen-Year-Olds* (London, National Children's Bureau).
8. Department of Education and Science (1978) *Special Educational Needs* (London, HMSO) p.1.
9. Fogelman (ed.) *Britain's Sixteen-Year-Olds*, p.29.
10. Department of Education and Science *Circular 2175*, p.3. For a discussion of the ascertainment process see Williams, P. (1965) 'The ascertainment of educationally subnormal children', *Educational Research*, vol. 7, no. 2, pp. 131–46.
11. Department of Education and Science, *Circular 2/75*.
12. Department of Education and Science, *Special Educational needs*, p.219.
13. Ibid, p.221.
14. Department of Education and Science, *Circular 15/70*.
15. Department of Education and Science, *Special Educational Needs*, p.38.
16. Ibid, p.38.
17. Provisional information supplied by DES.
18. Fogelman (ed.), *Britain's Sixteen-Year-Olds*, p.47.
19. For further details of these questionnaires and results from the most recent follow-up see ibid, pp.10–11.
20. Davie, *et al. From Birth to Seven*, p.162.
21. See Walker, A. and Lewis, P. (1977) 'Careers advice and employment references of a small group of handicapped school-leavers', *Careers Quarterly*, vol. 27, no. 1, pp.5–14.
22. The appendix is obtainable from The Supplementary Publications Division (Reference SUP 81009), British Library (Lending Division), Walton, Boston Spa, Wetherby, Yorkshire LS23 7BQ.
23. Ibid, Appendix A, Table A1.
24. Tuckey, *et al. Handicapped School Leavers*. p.14.
25. Maizels, J. (1970). *Adolescent needs and the Transition from School to Work* (London, Athlone Press) p.14.
26. A full report on this severely handicapped group has been written. Walker, A. and Lewis, P. (1977) 'School and post-school experiences of severely mentally handicapped young people'.

Chapter 4

1. See, for example, the comments of some employed men in an area of very high unemployment in Turner, S. and Dickinson, F. (1978) *In and Out of Work* (Newcastle-upon-Tyne, North Tyneside Community Development Project) chap. 9.
2. Centre for Policy Studies (1976) *What the July Employment Figures Really Show;* see also Lister, R. and Field, F. (1978) *Wasted Labour* (London, Child Poverty Action Group) p.75.
3. Brittan, S. (1975) *Second Thoughts on Full Employment Policy* (Chichester, Rose, for Centre for Policy Studies).
4. *Department of Employment Gazette,* vol. 87, no. 8, 1978.
8. Turner and Dickinson, *In and Out of Work* p.38 and chap. 6.
6. Townsend, P. (1979) 'The problem – an overview', in Barratt-Brown, M. *et al.* (eds.) *Full Employment* (Nottingham, Spokesman Books) p.12.
7. *Department of Employment Gazette,* vol. 87, no. 8, 1978, p.979; vol. 89, no. 8, 1980, p.900.
8. Manpower Services Commission (1977) *Young People and Work,* p.23.
9. Ibid, p.23.
10. Ibid, p.20.
11. Carter, M. (1966) *Into Work* (Harmondsworth, Penguin) p.134.
12. Supplementary table 4.1. Available from British Library (Lending Division). All subsequent references to this source will just indicate the table numbers.
13. See Reid, I. (1977) *Social Class Differences in Britain* (London, Open Books).
14. Ibid, p.23.
15. Office of Population Censuses and Surveys (1970) *Classification of Occupations* (London, HMSO).
16. Supplementary table 4.2.
17. Supplementary table 4.4.
18. Supplementary table 4.5.
19. Supplementary table 4.6.

Chapter 5

1. Lockwood, D. (1958) *The Blackcoated Worker* (London, Allen & Unwin) p.205.
2. Carter, M. (1966) *Into Work* (Harmondsworth, Penguin) p.169.
3. International Labour Organisation (1977) *Young People and Their Working Environment* (Geneva).
4. Lockwood, D. (1960) 'The new working class', *European Journal of Sociology,* vol. 1.
5. Supplementary table 5.1.
6. Maizels, J. (1970) *Adolescent Needs and the Transition from School to Work* (London, Athlone Press).
7. Liepmann, K. (1944) *The Journey to Work* (London, Routledge & Kegan Paul).
8. Supplementary table 5.2.
9. Supplementary table 5.3.
10. A similar list of facilities was used in the national survey of poverty: Townsend, P. (1979) *Poverty in the United Kingdom* (Harmondsworth, Penguin).

11. Supplementary table 5.4.
12. Brittan, A. (1977) *The Privatised World* (London, Routledge & Kegan Paul) esp. chap. 3.
13. Maizels, *Adolescent Needs and the Transition from School to Work.*
14. Handyside, J. D. (1961) 'Satisfaction and aspirations', *Occupational Psychology*, vol. 35, no. 4.
15. Supplementary table 5.5.
16. Supplementary table 5.6.
17. Supplementary table 5.7.
18. Supplementary table 5.8.
19. Supplementary table 5.9.
20. International Labour Office *Young People in Their Working Environment*, p.23.
21. Maizels, *Adolescent Needs and the Transition from School to Work*, p.204.
22. Ashton, D. N. and Field, D. (1976) *Young Workers* (London, Hutchinson) pp.100–1.
23. Supplementary table 5.10.
24. Carter, *Into Work*, p.165.
25. Supplementary table 5.11.
26. Supplementary table 5.12.
27. Supplementary table 5.13.
28. Thomas, R. and Wetherell, D. (1974) *Looking Forward to Work* (London, HMSO) p.335.
29. Fogelman, K. (ed.) *Britain's Sixteen-Year Olds* (London, National Children's Bureau) p.57.
30. Thomas and Wetherell, *Looking Forward to Work*, p.238.
31. Ibid, p.128.
32. Lockwood, D. (1966) 'Sources of variations in working class images of society', *Sociological Review*, vol. 14, pp.249–67; Goldthorpe, J. *et al.* (1968) *The Affluent Worker: Industrial Attitudes and Behaviour* (Cambridge University Press).
33. Thomas and Wetherell, *Looking Forward to Work*, p.128.
34. Lockwood, 'Sources of variations in working class images of society'.
35. Ashton and Field, *Young Workers*, chap. 3.
36. Fogelman (ed.), p.57.
37. Supplementary table 5.14.
38. Supplementary table 5.15.
39. Supplementary table 5.16.
40. Supplementary table 5.17.

Chapter 6

1. Fogelman, K. (ed.) (1976) *Britain's Sixteen-Year Olds* (London, National Children's Bureau) p.58.
2. Supplementary table 6.1.
3. Supplementary table 6.2.
4. Weir, A. D. and Nolan, F. J. (1977) *Glad to be Out?* (Edinburgh, Scottish Council for Research in Education) p.45.
5. Maizels, J. (1970) *Adolescent Needs and the Transition from School to Work* (London, Athlone Press) p.127.

6. Supplementary table 6.3.
7. Supplementary table 6.4.
8. Supplementary table 6.5.
9. Supplementary table 6.4.
10. Maizels, *Adolescent Needs and the Transition from School to Work,* p.126.
11. See, for example, Jahoda, G. (1952) 'Job attitudes and job choice among secondary school leavers', *Occupational Psychology,* vol. 26, nos. 3–4; Veness, T. (1962) *School Leavers: their Aspirations and Expectations* (London, Methuen); Carter, M. P. (1962) *Home, School and Work* (Oxford, Pergamon) chap. 6.
12. Moor, C. H. (1976) *From School to Work* (London, Sage) p.74.
13. Carter, *Home, School and Work,* p.135.
14. Weir and Nolan, *Glad to be Out?,* p.33.
15. Supplementary table 6.6.
16. Carter, M. (1966) *Into Work* (Harmondsworth, Penguin) p.110.
17. Supplementary table 6.7.
18. Supplementary table 6.8.
19. Supplementary table 6.9.
20. Supplementary table 6.10.
21. Carter, *Into Work,* p.110.
22. Supplementary table 6.12.
23. Supplementary table 6.13.
24. Supplementary table 6.14.
25. Supplementary table 6.15.
26. Supplementary table 6.16.
27. Ashton, D. N. and Field, D. (1977) *Young Workers* (London, Hutchinson) chap. 3.
28. Thomas, R. and Wetherell, D. (1974) *Looking forward to Work* (London, HMSO) pp.169–70 (my emphasis in last sentence).
29. Ibid, p.170.
30. Ibid.

Chapter 7

1. Roberts, K. (1977) 'The social conditions, consequences and limitations of careers guidance', *British Journal of Guidance and Counselling,* vol. 5, no. 1, p.6.
2. Ginzberg, E. *et al.* (1951) *Occupational Choice* (New York, Columbia University Press); Super, D. E. *et al.* (1957) *Vocational Development* (New York, Columbia University Press).
3. Musgrave, P. W. (1974) 'Towards a sociological theory of occupational choice' in Williams, W. M. (ed.) *Occupational Choice* (London, Allen & Unwin) chap. 4.
4. Roberts, K. (1968) 'The entry into employment: an approach towards a general theory', *Sociological Review,* vol. 16, no. 2, p.177; Keil, E. T. *et al.* (1966) ·Youth and work: problems and perspectives', *Sociological Review,* vol. 14, no. 2.
5. Thomas, R. and Wetherell, D. (1974) *Looking Forward to Work* (London, HMSO) p.239.

6. Sofer, C. (1974) 'Introduction', in Williams, W. M. (ed.), *Occupational Choice* (London, Allen & Unwin) p.31.

7. Thomas, R. and Wetherell, D. (1974) *Looking Forward to Work*, p.170.

8. Supplementary table 7.1.

9. Ferguson, T. and Kerr, A. W. (1960) *Handicapped Youth* (London, Oxford University Press) p.28.

10. Supplementary table 7.2.

11. Supplementary table 7.3.

12. Supplementary table 7.4.

13. Supplementary table 7.5.

14. Supplementary table 7.6.

15. Supplementary table 7.7.

16. Supplementary table 7.8.

17. Supplementary table 7.9.

18. Supplementary table 7.10.

19. Supplementary table 7.11.

20. Supplementary table 7.12.

21. Supplementary table 7.13.

22. Supplementary table 7.14.

23. Supplementary tables 7.15, 7.16.

24. Supplementary table 7.17.

25. Department of Education and Science (1973) *Careers Education in Secondary Schools* (London, HMSO) p.61.

26. Horton-Williams, R. *et al.* (1968) *Young School Leavers* (London, HMSO).

27. Kirton, M. *et al.* (1976) *Careers Knowledge of Sixth Form Boys* (London, Careers and Occupational Information Centre) p.68.

28. Thomas and Wetherell, *Looking Forward to Work*, chap.9.

29. Fogelman, K. (ed.) (1976) *Britain's Sixteen-Year-Olds* (London, National Children's Bureau) p.42.

30. Lambert, L. (1978) 'Careers guidance and choosing a job', *British Journal of Guidance and Counselling*, vol. 6, no. 2, pp.147–60.

31. Hanson, A. (1976) *Reading to Leave* (London, Collins).

Chapter 8

1. Supplementary table 8.1.

2. Supplementary table 8.2.

3. Supplementary table 8.3.

4. Supplementary table 8.4.

5. Supplementary table 8.5.

6. Supplementary table 8.6.

7. Supplementary table 8.7.

8. Supplementary table 8.8.

9. Supplementary table 8.9.

10. Supplementary table 8.10.

11. Supplementary table 8.11.

12. Supplementary table 8.12.

13. Supplementary table 8.13.

14. Supplementary table 8.14.

15. Supplementary table 8.15.
16. Supplementary table 8.16.
17. Supplementary table 8.17.
18. Supplementary table 8.18.
19. In some cases where NCDS data were used sample numbers were reduced because of a low response rate to certain questions in the previous follow-ups. In all cases percentages are calculated on the basis of the number for whom data were available.
20. Supplementary table 8.20.
21. Supplementary table 8.21.
22. Supplementary table 8.22.
23. Supplementary table 8.23.
24. Supplementary table 8.24.
25. Supplementary table 8.25.
26. Supplementary table 8.26.
27. Supplementary table 8.27.
28. Supplementary table 8.28.
29. Supplementary table 8.29.

Chapter 9

1. See Maizels, J. (1970) *Adolescent Needs and the Transition from School to Work* (London, Athlone Press); and Veness, T. (1962) *School Leavers, their Aspirations and Expectations* (London, Methuen).
2. Carter, M. (1966) *Into Work* (Harmondsworth, Penguin) p.158.
3. Supplementary table 9.1.
4. Ferguson, T. and Cunnison, J. (1951) *The Young Wage Earner* (Oxford University Press).
5. Central Advisory Council for Education (1959) *15 to 18* (London, HMSO) vol. 11.
6. Hill, M. J. (1975) 'Unstable employment in the histories of unemployed men', *IMS Monitor,* vol. 3, no. 2; Daniel, W. (1974) *A National Survey of the Unemployed* (London, PEP).
7. Supplementary table 9.2.
8. Supplementary table 9.3.
9. Supplementary table 9.4.
10. Supplementary table 9.5.
11. Supplementary table 9.6.
12. Supplementary table 9.7.
13. Supplementary table 9.8.
14. Supplementary table 9.9.
15. Supplementary table 9.10.
16. Supplementary table 9.11.
17. Supplementary table 9.12.
18. Supplementary table 9.13.
19. Supplementary table 9.14.
20. Supplementary table 9.15.
21. Supplementary table 9.16.
22. Supplementary table 9.17.

23. Supplementary table 9.18.
24. As with the similar section in the previous chapter, analysis of some of the following variables was limited by the availability of NCDS data on the respondents. Therefore, in some cases numbers in each sample group were reduced.
25. Supplementary table 9.19.
26. Supplementary table 9.20.
27. Hill, J. (1978) 'The psychological impact of unemployment', *New Society,* vol. 43, no. 798, pp.118–20.
28. Supplementary table 9.21.
29. Supplementary table 9.22.
30. Supplementary table 9.23. Although 28 per cent of the maladjusted sample were receiving help at 16 for behaviour difficulties, 35 per cent of the ESN(M), 29 per cent of the physically handicapped and 78 per cent of the ESN(S) were also receiving such help in school.
31. Supplementary table 9.24.
32. Supplementary table 9.25.
33. Supplementary table 9.26.
34. Supplementary table 9.27.
35. Supplementary table 9.28.
36. Supplementary table 9.30.
37. Supplementary table 9.31.
38. Supplementary table 9.32. These figures apply only to those who had worked since leaving school rather than the full sample discussed above.
39. Supplementary table 9.33.
40. Gordon, D. M. (1972) *Economic Theories of Poverty and Underemployment* (Lexington, Mass., D. C. Heath) p.6.
41. Ibid, p.7.
42. Liebow, E. (1967) *Tally's Corner* (London, Routledge & Kegan Paul).
43. Hall, R. E. (1970) 'Why is the unemployment rate so high at full employment?', *Brookings Papers on Economic Activity,* no. 3.
44. Bluestone, B. (1970) 'The tripartite economy: labour markets and the working poor', *Poverty and Human Resources,* July–August 1970; Doeringer, P. B. and Piore, M. J. (1971) *Internal Labour Markets and Manpower Analysis* (Lexington, Mass., D. C. Heath).
45. Supplementary table 9.34.
46. Phillips, D. (1973) 'Young and unemployed in a northern city', Weir, D. (ed.), *Men and Work in Modern Britain* (London, Fontana) p.417.
47. Jackson, R. N. (1968) 'Employment adjustment of educable mentally handicapped school-leavers', in Association for Special Education, *The Child and the Outside World* (London, ASE) pp.131–7.
48. Gunzberg, E. *et al.* (1951) *Occupational Choice* (New York, Columbia University Press).
49. Carter, M. (1975) 'Teenage workers: a second chance at 18?', in Brannen, P. (ed.), *Entering the World of Work: Some Sociological Perspectives* (London, HMSO) p.104; see also Carter, *Into Work,* pp.158–64.

Chapter 10

1. Department of Employment (1974) *Unqualified, Untrained and Unemployed – Report of a Working Party set up by the National Youth Employment Council* (London, HMSO) p.21.
2. Ibid, p.22.
3. Ibid, p.22.
4. Ibid, p.65; for discussion of the apathy associated with long-term employment see Marsden, D. and Duff, E. (1975) *Workless* (Harmondsworth, Penguin) chap. 9; and Turner, S. and Dickinson, F. (1978) *In and Out of Work* (Newcastle-upon-Tyne, North Tyneside Community Development Project) chap. 9.
5. CBI *Memorandum*, December 1976, p.1.
6. See, for example, Engineering Employers Federation (1975) *Comments on Vocation Preparation for Young People*.
7. Apprentices taught basic maths *(The Times*, 18 February 1977).
8. See Bowles, S. and Gintis, H. (1972) 'IQ in the US class structure', *Social Policy*, Nov–Dec, p.83.
9. Ibid, p.83. For an example of how this operates at one end of the class structure see Stanworth, P. and Giddens, A. (eds) (1974) *Elites and Power in British Society* (Cambridge University Press).
10. Gellman, W. (1959) 'Roots of prejudice against the handicapped', *Journal of Rehabilitation*, vol. 23, no. 1, pp.4–6; Olshansky, S. and Unterberger, H. (1965) 'Employer prejudice against the mentally retarded', *Journal of Rehabilitation*, vol. 31, no. 5, pp.23–4.
11. Nagi, S. Z. *et al.* (1962) 'Work, employment and the disabled', *American Journal of Economics and Sociology*, vol. 6, p.23.
12. See MIND (1978) *Nobody Wants You: 40 Cases of Discrimination at Work*.
13. Ullman, A. and Davis, M. S. (1965) 'Assessing the medical patient's motivation and ability to work', *Social Casework*, vol. 46, pp.195–202.
14. Wansbrough, N. (1973) 'From psychiatric ward to shopfloor', *New Society*, vol. 24, no. 50, pp.128–31.
15. Behrand, H. (1959) 'Financial incentives as the expression of a system of beliefs', *British Journal of Sociology*, vol. 10, pp.137–47.
16. Ibid, p.138.
17. See Lowman, P. (1974) 'The sub-normal employee', *Management Today*, October 1974, pp.35–40.
18. Institute of Manpower Studies (1975) *People and Jobs in Distribution; a report to the Distributive Industry Training Board* (Manchester, Training Board).
19. Olshansky, S. *et al.* (1958) 'Employers' attitudes and practices on the hiring of ex-mental patients', *Mental Hygiene*, vol. 42, no. 3, pp.391–401.

Chapter 11

1. Floud, J. *et al.* (1956) *Social Class and Educational Opportunity* (London, Heinemann); Little, A. and Westergaard, J. (1964) 'The trend of class differentials in educational opportunity in England and Wales', *British Journal of Sociology*, vol. 15, pp.301–16.
2. Department of Education and Science (1978) *Primary Education in England* (London, HMSO).

3. Berg, I. (1973) *Education and Jobs* (Harmondsworth, Penguin).
4. Maizels, J. (1970) *Adolescent Needs and the Transition from School to Work* (London, Athlone Press) pp.232–6; Carter, M. (1966) *Into Work* (Harmondsworth, Penguin) p.195.
5. Ibid, p.229.
6. For example, see Tuckey, L. *et al.* (1973) *Handicapped School Leavers* (Windsor, NFER).
7. Inner London Education Authority (1975) *Provision for Handicapped Students in Further and Higher Education*, p.9.
8. Training Services Agency (1975) *Vocational Preparation for Young People* (London, Manpower Services Commission) p.12.
9. Department of Education and Science (1973) *Adult Education: A Plan for Development* (London, HMSO) p.9.
10. Supplementary table 11.1.
11. Supplementary table 11.2.
12. Supplementary table 11.3.
13. Supplementary table 11.4.
14. Supplementary table 11.5.
15. Supplementary table 11.6.
16. Supplementary table 11.7.
17. Weir, D. and Nolan, F. (1977) *Glad to be Out?* (Edinburgh, Scottish Council for Research in Education) pp.83–4.
18. Maizels, *Adolescent Needs and the Transition from School to Work* p.224.; see also Carter, *Into Work*, pp.182–84.
19. Department of Employment (1974) *Unqualified, Untrained and Unemployed: Report of a Working Party set up by the National Youth Employment Council* (London, HMSO) p.23.
20. Liepmann, K. (1960) *Apprenticeship* (London, HMSO); Carter, *Into Work*, p.182.
21. Supplementary table 11.3.
22. Maizels, *Adolescent Needs and the Transition from School to Work*, p.225; Training Services Agency, *Vocational Preparation for Young People*, p.7.
23. MRC, *Young School Leavers at Work and College. Report submitted to SSRC, 1971.*
24. Supplementary table 11.11.
25. Supplementary table 11.12.
26. Supplementary table 11.13.
27. Supplementary table 11.14.
28. Institute of Manpower Services (1975) *People and Jobs in Distribution: a report to the Distributive Industry Training Board* (Manchester, The Training Board).
29. Ibid.
30. Department of Education and Science (1964) *Day Release* (London, HMSO) p.16.
31. Weir and Nolan, *Glad to be Out?*, p.84.
32. Department of Education and Science, *Adult Education: A Plan for Development*, p.8.
33. Department of Education and Science, *Primary Education in England*. It is ironic that parents in the manual-class are contributing a greater proportion of taxation and their children benefit less than those parents in non-manual

classes. See Glennerster, H. (1972) 'Education and inequality' in Townsend, P. and Bosanquet, N. (eds), *Labour and Inequality* (London, Fabian Society) pp.83–107.

34. Berg, *Education and Jobs* (chaps 2, 3 and 5.) See also 'Good Marks Teacher', *Guardian*, 27 September 1978.

35. Community Relations Commission (1976) *A Second Chance*.

Chapter 12

1. First drafted by Patricia Stapenhurst.
2. See p.12 and references.
3. Tuckey, L. *et al.* (1973) *Handicapped School Leavers* (Windsor, NFER).
4. Davie, R. *et al.* (1972) *From Birth to Seven* (London, Longman).
5. See, for example, DES *Circular* 5/74.
6. Ministry of Health (1968) *Local Authority Training Centres for Mentally Handicapped Adults: Model of Good Practice* (London, HMSO).
7. Walker, A. and Lewis, P. (1977) 'School and Post-School Experiences of a Sample of Severely Mentally Handicapped Young People', mimeo.
8. Ibid, p.80.

Chapter 13

1. Central Advisory Council for Education (1967) *Children and Their Primary Schools* (London, HMSO) vol. 11; see also Floud, J. (ed.) (1956) *Social Class and Educational Opportunity* (London, Heinemann); Musgrove, F. (1966) *The Family, Education and Society* (London, Routledge & Kegan Paul); Douglas, J. W. B. (1964) *The Home and the School* (London, MacGibbon & Kee); Wiseman, S. (1964) *Education and Environment* (Manchester University Press).
2. Supplementary table 13.1.
3. Supplementary table 13.2.
4. Supplementary table 13.3.
5. The 'three-day week' was in progress at the time of the third NCDS follow-up.
6. Supplementary table 13.4.
7. Carter, M. (1966) *Into Work* (Harmondsworth, Penguin) p.110.
8. Ibid, p.111.
9. Bynner, J. M. (1972) *Parents' Attitudes to Education* (London, HMSO).
10. Ibid, p.1.
11. Central Advisory Council for Education, *Children and Their Primary Schools*.
12. Supplementary table 13.5A.
13. Supplementary table 13.5B.
14. Supplementary table 13.6.
15. Supplementary table 13.7.
16. Supplementary table 13.8.
17. Supplementary table 13.9.
18. Supplementary table 13.10.
19. It is possible that this results from social class differences in the use of the terms 'English' and 'reading, writing and spelling'.
20. Supplementary table 13.11.

21. Supplementary table 13.12. Handicapped *vs* non-handicapped: $X^2 = 46.9$, 6 degrees of freedom, $p < 0.001$.
22. Supplementary table 13.13.
23. Bynner, *Parents' Attitudes to Education*, p.15.
24. Supplementary table 13.14.
25. Supplementary table 13.15.
26. Supplementary table 13.16.
27. Excluding ESN(S) $p < 0.001$ $X^2 = 31.1$, 10 degrees of freedom.
28. Excluding ESN(S) $p < 0.001$ $X^2 = 26.6$, 10 degrees of freedom.
29. Supplementary table 13.17.
30. Supplementary table 13.18.

Chapter 14

1. Bosanquet, N. and Standing, G. (1972) 'Government and unemployment 1966–70: a study of policy and evidence', *British Journal of Industrial Relations*, vol. 10, no. 2.
2. Turner, S. and Dickinson, F. (1978) *In and Out of Work* (Newcastle-upon-Tyne, North Tyneside Community Development Project) chaps 11–17; Lister, R. and Field, F. (1978) *Wasted Labour* (London, Child Poverty Action Group) chaps 3–4.
3. Office of Population Censuses and Surveys (1973) *General Household Survey* (London, HMSO).
4. Sinfield, A. (1968) *The Long-Term Unemployed* (Paris, OECD) p.30; Hill, M. J. *et al.* (1973) *Men Out of Work* (Cambridge University Press) pp.10–11.
5. See, for example, Williams, W. M. (ed.) (1974) *Occupational Choice* (London, Allen & Unwin).
6. See, for example, Veness, T. (1962) *School Leavers: their Aspirations and Expectations* (London, Methuen).
7. British Youth Council (1977) *Youth Unemployment: Causes and Cures*, p.25.
8. Millham, S. (1977) *Springboard Sunderland* (London, Community Service Volunteers).
9. Floud, J. (ed.) (1956) *Social Class and Educational Opportunity* (London, Heinemann); Craft, M. (ed.) (1970) *Family, Class and Education* (London, Longman).
10. Lindsay, K. (1926) *Social Progress and Educational Waste* (London, Routledge & Kegan Paul).
11. Central Advisory Council for Education (1959) *15 to 18* (London, HMSO); Committee on Higher Education (1968) *Higher Education Report* (London, HMSO); Douglas, J. W. B. *et al.* (1968) *All Our Future* (London, Peter Davies).
12. Craft (ed.), p.4.
13. See Mogey, J. (1956) *Family and Neighbourhood* (Oxford University Press); Sweig, F. (1961) *The Worker in an Affluent Society* (London, Heinemann).
14. Marsden, D. (1967) 'School, class and the parents' dilemma', in Mabey, R. (ed.) *Class* (London, Blond) p.38.
15. Morton-Williams, R. *et al.* (1968) *Young School Leavers* (London, HMSO) p.195.

16. Hunt, S. M. (1975) *Parents of the 'ESN'* (Manchester, National Elfrida Rathbone Society) p.5.
17. Bosanquet, N. (1973) *Race and Employment in Britain* (London, Runnymede Trust) p.8.
18. Rutter, M. *et al.* (1979) *Fifteen Thousand Hours* (London, Open Books).
19. Beinstein, B. (1970) 'Education cannot compensate for society', *New Society*, 26 Feb 1970.
20. Tawney, R. H. (1966) *The Radical Tradition* (Harmondsworth, Penguin) p.52.
21. Walker, A. (forthcoming) 'Which way for the careers service?'.
22. See Simon, M. (1977) *Youth in Industry* (Leicester, National Youth Bureau) pp.60–1.
23. National Economic Development Office (1972) *What the Girls Think*, p.15.
24. Weir, M. (ed.) (1976) *Job Satisfaction* (London, Fontana).
25. Reported in Weir, M. (1976), *Redesigning Jobs in Scotland* (Work Research Unit).
26. Industrial Training Research Unit (1974) *Versatility at Work;* see also Blake, J. and Ross, S. 'Some experiences with autonomous work groups' in Weir, M. (ed.) *Job Satisfaction*, pp.185–93.
27. Wilson, W. A. B. (1973) *On the Quality of Working Life* (London, HMSO); Hughes, J. and Gregory, D. (1974) 'Richer jobs for workers', *New Society*, vol. 27, no. 593, pp.386–7; Weir, M. (ed.) (1976) *Job Satisfaction*.
28. Ferman, L. (1969) *Job-Development for the Hard-to-Employ* (Michigan, Institute of Labour and Industrial Relations) p.4.
29. Ibid, p.43.
30. Ibid, p.13. (1969)
31. Quoted in Carter, M. (1966) *Into Work* (Harmondsworth, Penguin) p.169.
32. Ferman, *Job-Development for the Hard-to-Employ*, p.42.

Index